WILLIAM

SHAKESPEARE'S

VERILY, A NEW HOPE

WILLIAM
SHAKESPEARE'S

![STAR WARS](STAR WARS logo)

VERILY, A NEW HOPE

By Ian Doescher

INSPIRED BY THE WORK OF GEORGE LUCAS
AND WILLIAM SHAKESPEARE

QUIRK BOOKS
PHILADELPHIA

Library of Congress Cataloging in Publication Number: 2012953985

ISBN: 978-1-59474-637-6

Printed in the United States of America

Typeset in Sabon and Trajan

Designed by Doogie Horner
Text by Ian Doescher
Illustrations by Nicolas Delort
Production management by John J. McGurk

Quirk Books
215 Church Street
Philadelphia, PA 19106
quirkbooks.com

10 9 8 7

TO GRAHAM AND LIAM,

MY YOUNG PADAWANS,

AND JENNIFER, "BUT NEVER

DOUBT I LOVE . . . "

DRAMATIS PERSONAE

CHORUS

LUKE SKYWALKER, *a boy of Tatooine*
OWEN LARS, *his uncle*
BERU LARS, *his aunt*
OBI-WAN KENOBI, *a Jedi knight*
PRINCESS LEIA ORGANA, *of Alderaan*
HAN SOLO, *a smuggler*
CHEWBACCA, *a Wookiee and Han's first mate*
DARTH VADER, *a Sith Lord*
GOVERNOR TARKIN, *of the Imperial army*
C-3PO, *a droid*
R2-D2, *his companion*
JABBA THE HUTT, *a boss*
GREEDO, *his bounty hunter*
WEDGE ANTILLES, *a rebel pilot*
BIGGS DARKLIGHTER, *a rebel pilot*

REBEL LEADERS, CHIEF PILOTS, STORMTROOP-
ERS, CAPTAINS, COMMANDERS, ADMIRALS,
GUARDS, JAWAS, DROIDS, TUSKEN RAIDERS, BAR
PATRONS, IMPERIAL LEADERS, *and* REBEL PILOTS

PROLOGUE.

Outer space.

Enter CHORUS.

CHORUS   It is a period of civil war.
              The spaceships of the rebels, striking swift
              From base unseen, have gain'd a vict'ry o'er
              The cruel Galactic Empire, now adrift.
              Amidst the battle, rebel spies prevail'd   5
              And stole the plans to a space station vast,
              Whose pow'rful beams will later be unveil'd
              And crush a planet: 'tis the DEATH STAR blast.
              Pursu'd by agents sinister and cold,
              Now Princess Leia to her home doth flee,   10
              Deliv'ring plans and a new hope they hold:
              Of bringing freedom to the galaxy.
              In time so long ago begins our play,
              In star-crossed galaxy far, far away.

                                        [Exit.

ACT I

SCENE 1.

Aboard the rebel ship.

Enter C-3PO and R2-D2.

C-3PO	Now is the summer of our happiness
	Made winter by this sudden, fierce attack!
	Our ship is under siege, I know not how.
	O hast thou heard? The main reactor fails!
	We shall most surely be destroy'd by this. 5
	I'll warrant madness lies herein!
R2-D2	—Beep beep,
	Beep, beep, meep, squeak, beep, beep, beep, whee!
C-3PO	—We're doomed.
	The princess shall have no escape this time!
	I fear this battle doth portend the end
	Of the Rebellion. O! What misery! 10

[Exeunt C-3PO and R2-D2.

CHORUS	Now watch, amaz'd, as swiftly through the door
	The army of the Empire flyeth in.
	And as the troopers through the passage pour,
	They murder sev'ral dozen rebel men.

[Fighting begins.

Enter REBELS. *Many die. Enter* STORMTROOPERS *and* DARTH VADER.
Exeunt. Enter R2-D2 *with* PRINCESS LEIA. C-3PO *is across
the stage.*

C-3PO	Pray, R2-D2, where art thou?

[Exit Princess Leia.

R2-D2   —Beep, meep.   15

C-3PO   At last, where hast thou been? I fear they come
          In this direction. Pray, what shall we do?
          My circuitry o'erloads, my mind's o'erthrown!
          And fear hath put its grip into my wires.
          We shall be sent unto that place I dread—   20
          The Kessel spice mines whence no droid returns—
          And there be blasted into who knows what!

                              [R2-D2 begins to exit.

          Anon, anon, R2! Where dost thou go?
          O prithee, patience, leave me not alone.
          [*Aside:*] Aye, even though I mock and injure thee,   25
          I'll surely die if e'er thou leavest me!

                              [Exeunt droids.

SCENE 2.

Aboard the rebel ship.

Enter DARTH VADER, *carrying* REBEL LEADER 1 *by the neck,*
and STORMTROOPERS.

TROOPER 1 The Death Star plans we could not find herein,
           Nor are they on the main computer, Lord.
           In short, they are not here, and there's an end.

VADER   Thou speakest well, my stormtrooper, and yet
           Not well upon my ear the message falls.   5
           I turn to thee, thou rebel. Aye, I lift
           Thy head above my own. Thou canst now choose

To keep thy secrets lock'd safe in that head,
And therefore lose the life thou holdest dear,
Or else to keep thy head and, thus, thy life.   10
My patience runneth quickly out much like
The sands across the dunes of Tatooine.
So tell me, else thou diest quick: where shall
We find transmissions thou didst intercept?
What hast thou done, say, with those plans?
        [Darth Vader begins to choke Rebel Leader 1.
REBEL 1   —My Lord,   15
My head and life I value—certain 'tis!
And yet to thee I must report we have
Not intercepted one transmission! Ahh!
This is a cons'lar ship, and nothing more,
On diplomatic mission. Ugh!
VADER   —Thou knave!   20
With thy last breath hear thou this word: if this
Is but a cons'lar ship, then where is the
ambassador? [*Rebel Leader 1 dies.*] Commander,
                        prithee, go!
Rend thou this ship apart until the plans
Are found, and bring me any passengers—   25
Upon thy life, I want them brought alive!
                        [*Exeunt stormtroopers.*
And so another dies by my own hand,
This hand, which now encas'd in blackness is.
O that the fingers of this wretched hand
Had not the pain of suff'ring ever known.   30
But now my path is join'd unto the dark,
And wicked men—whose hands and fingers move

To crush their foes—are now my company.
So shall my fingers ever undertake
To do more evil, aye, and this—my hand—   35
Shall do the Emp'ror's bidding evermore.
And thus we see how fingers presage death
And hands become the instruments of Fate.

          [Exit Darth Vader.

Enter STORMTROOPERS, *searching. Enter* PRINCESS LEIA,
       holding a blaster.

TROOPER 1 Aye, there is one. My comrades, set for stun!
      [Princess Leia shoots, Stormtrooper 1 dies.
        Stormtroopers stun Princess Leia.
TROOPER 2 She shall be well. Go now, inform the dread   40
      Lord Vader we have caught a prisoner.
      [Aside:] And may Mos Eisley drinks flow swift and
      free
      When Vader grants rewards for work well done!
      [Exeunt stormtroopers with Princess Leia.

Enter C-3PO *and* R2-D2 *as the latter enters escape pod.*

C-3PO   Hold! Thou art not permitted to go in.
      Deactivated thou shalt surely be.   45
R2-D2   Beep, beep, beep, meep!
C-3PO   —Thou shalt not label me
      A mindless, brute philosopher! Nay, nay,
      Thou overladen glob of grease, thou imp,
      Thou rubbish bucket fit for scrap, thou blue

And silver pile of bantha dung! Now, come,   50
And get thee hence away lest someone sees.

R2-D2   Beep, meep, beep, squeak, beep, beep, beep, meep,
                                        beep, whee!

C-3PO   What secret mission? And what plans? What dost
                    Thou talk about? I'll surely not get in!
                                        [Sound of blast.
                    I warrant I'll regret this. So say I!   55
                              [Exit C-3PO into escape pod.

R2-D2   This golden droid has been a friend, 'tis true,
                    And yet I wish to still his prating tongue!
                    An imp, he calleth me? I'll be reveng'd,
                    And merry pranks aplenty I shall play
                    Upon this pompous droid C-3PO!   60
                    Yet not in language shall my pranks be done:
                    Around both humans and the droids I must
                    Be seen to make such errant beeps and squeaks
                    That they shall think me simple. Truly, though,
                    Although with sounds oblique I speak to them,   65
                    I clearly see how I shall play my part,
                    And how a vast rebellion shall succeed
                    By wit and wisdom of a simple droid.
                              [Exit R2-D2 into escape pod.

CHORUS   Now climb the metal pair into the pod,
                    Which shooteth from the ship like laser blast.   70
                    And to the planet's face, as straight as rod,
                    The capsule takes the droids by power vast.

Enter CHIEF PILOT *and* CAPTAIN.

PILOT   There strays another one.
CAPTAIN   —Pray, hold thy fire:
                For certain there are no life forms aboard.
                And truly what may be the chance that aught   75
                But life alone could fly within that pod?
                The rebels could not be so cunning bold
                To put the Death Star plans therein. If I
                Were one to bet, I'd stake my life on it!
                All's well that endeth well, so say the wise,   80
                And so that pod shall live to land below.
                            [Exeunt chief pilot and captain.

                    Enter DROIDS, aside in escape pod.

C-3PO   'Tis but a jest—aye surely, we are mock'd!
                For R2-D2, plainly canst thou see
                The damage looks but minor from below.
                Can thou be sure this pod is safe?
R2-D2   —Beep.
C-3PO   —O.   85
                                            [Exeunt.

SCENE 3.
Aboard the rebel ship.

Enter DARTH VADER and STORMTROOPERS with PRINCESS LEIA.

LEIA   Darth Vader, only thou couldst be so bold.
                When first my ship was under siege, I knew

'Twas thee who had this peaceful vessel sack'd.
Th'Imperi'l Senate shall not stand for this.
For when they hear thou hast attack'd a ship   5
On diplomatic mission—

VADER   —Highness, peace!
Be thou not so surpris'd. For well thou knowst
A mercy mission this was not, this time.
Thine innocent appearance doth disguise
A heart with revolution at its core.   10
Aye, several transmissions were there beam'd
Unto this ship by rebel spies. I want
To know what happen'd to the plans they sent!
And prithee, speak thou well, or speak thy last,
For fairer necks than thine my hand hath crush'd.   15

LEIA   Thine idle threat is meaningless to me.
My neck, my tongue, my mouth—these instruments
Of speech have not the power to relate
The knowledge that thou seek'st. For certain 'tis
I nothing know of what thou ask of me.   20
For I am but a member of the great
Imperi'l Senate, bound for Alderaan
On mission diplomatic.

VADER   —Nay, thou liest!
For thou art with the reb'l alliance vile,
And worse, a traitor! Take this one away!   25

       [*Exeunt stormtroopers with Princess Leia.*
The blood and wires within me leap with fire
When all these trait'rous words I must endure.

       Enter COMMANDER.

COMMAND. Lord, holding her is dangerous. If word
            Of this is told, then sympathy may rise
            For the Rebellion in the Senate's mind.   30
            So shall our pow'r o'er all the universe
            Be weaken'd by this wicked, cunning wretch.
            'Tis like the tale my mother told me once
            Of bygone emperor whose reign was lost
            When putrid Ugnaughts rose against his throne.   35
            So hath my mother said, and I with her:
            A deathly blow oft comes from tiny fist,
            And greatest tree may fall by smallest axe.

VADER   Commander, peace, and trouble not thy mind
            With tales of old. The princess shall reveal   40
            Her treachery when all's to do is done.
            The rebel spies are aptly traced to her,
            And now is she my only link to find
            The hidden rebel base.

COMMAND.   —I'll wager she
            Will die ere she tells thee.

VADER   —Leave that to me.   45
            Now go, be on thy way, and take this task:
            Send thou a signal of distress, and then
            Inform the Senate all aboard were kill'd.
            So shall our presence here be hid from sight,
            And thus our swift attack shall not be known.   50

Enter CAPTAIN.

CAPTAIN   Lord Vader, sorry am I to report:
            There are no battle plans aboard this ship,

And neither were transmissions made. There was
But one escape pod jettison'd amid
The fighting. But no life forms were aboard.   55
For certain 'twas a harmless accident.

VADER   With purpose rank must she have quickly hid
           The plans in the escape pod.

CAPTAIN   —Woman vile!
           Howe'er could she deceive my subtle mind?
           The plans in the escape pod! O, most rare!   60

VADER   Pray, cease thy speech and mark ye what I say:
           Take thou a keen and swift detachment down,
           And bring me back the plans. Commander, go!
           See to the task thyself, before the chime—
           There shall be none to stop our plan this time!   65

                                           [Exeunt.

SCENE 4.

The desert planet Tatooine.

CHORUS   And now, dear viewers, shall our play go to
           A planet stark and drear for our next scene.
           Imagine sand and rocks within thy view.
           Prepare thy souls—we fly to Tatooine!

                  Enter C-3PO and R2-D2.

C-3PO   Forsooth, how did we get into this mess?   5
           I tell thee verily, I know not how.
           A thousand tauntaun bow'ls could not produce

A greater desecration than this place.
Alas, we two are made for suffering—
I fear, R2, 'tis but our lot in life.   10
More than six million forms of speech I know,
Yet not a one shall help me now.

R2-D2   —Beep, beep.

C-3PO   Now must I rest before I come apart,
My joints are nearly frozen! Aye, I freeze!
For 'tis as though the vicious cold of death   15
Hath sunken deep into my circuitry.
O what a desolate terrain this is!

                    [R2-D2 begins to depart.

R2-D2   Beep, beep, beep, whistle, beep, beep, meep, beep,
                                    beep!

C-3PO   Where dost thou think thou goest?

R2-D2   —Beep, beep, beep!
[*Aside:*] Now shall I leave his company awhile—   20
Belike my absence shall alleviate
His obstinate resolve, and teach him thoughts
Of kindness, care and good humility.

C-3PO   Well I shall not go thither with thee, droid!
'Tis far too rocky. Canst thou not perceive?   25
Nay, truly. For the sun upon thy cold
And hard exterior hath surely warp'd
Thine often prudent mind. Pray, understand:
The road herein is better far. Why dost
Thou think that settlements will be found yon?   30

R2-D2   Beep, beep.

C-3PO   —Be thou not technical with me,
Or else thine input valve may swift receive

A hearty helping of my golden foot.

R2-D2   Beep, squeak.

                —What mission? What dost thou speak

                                    of?

R2-D2   Squeak, squeak, beep.

C-3PO   —More of thee I shall not take.   35

So, go thou hence! Thou shalt malfunction ere

The day is through, nearsighted pile of scrap!

Now may'st thou travel hence upon thy way

And find thy mission in a sarlacc pit!

Then shalt thou know for lo, these thousand years,   40

The pain I suffer as thy counterpart!

And be thou not behind me, arrant knave.

Aye, mark me—follow not, nor seek thou help,

For thou no satisfaction shalt receive.

R2-D2   Beep, beep, beep, meep. Beep, beep, beep, squeak,

                                  squeak, squeak!   45

C-3PO   No more with thine adventures! I go not

Upon thy way. [*R2-D2 exits.*] Malfunctioning small

                                    fool!

'Tis all his fault. He trick'd me so that I

Should go this way. But he shall not fare well.

O gods above, why have I once again   50

Been short with R2, sending him away?

I trust he knoweth well I hold him dear,

Though in his presence oft my speech is cruel.

'Tis words that do betray my better self

When harshly they express my droidly rage.   55

And yet for protocol I'm made, and must

With words fulfill my task. So then 'tis true

That words are both my ruin and my strength.
And yet—although I find myself adrift
And lost within a speechless sea of sand—   60
This word is true if ever words have truth:
Forever lost I'd be should I lose him.
But wait, what's that? A transport! Saved am I!
Hark, over here! Hey nonny non! Please help!

                                         [C-3PO exits.

CHORUS   A vessel vast comes forth across the sand,   65
And takes C-3PO within its hold.
But what of R2-D2's mission grand?
How doth the tale of this small droid unfold?

Enter R2-D2 and JAWAS, *hidden.*

R2-D2   Beep, ooh, beep, beep, beep, squeak.
JAWA 1   —Peska bahman.
Te peska bahman. Fuligiliha!   70
R2-D2   Ahh! Beep, beep, squeak, beep, beep, ahh!

                         [Jawas stun R2-D2, who falls.

JAWA 2   —Utinni!

                   [Jawas carry R2-D2 into transport.

CHORUS   Imagine now that on this stage you see
Full many droids and creatures quite bizarre.
And yet, amid this ghastly company,
Herein the two friends reunited are.   75

Enter other DROIDS *and* C-3PO.

C-3PO   Good R2? R2-D2, O 'tis thee!

R2-D2   Beep, beep, beep, whistle, squeak, beep, meep, beep,
                                                    whee!
                                              [Exeunt.

SCENE 5.
The desert planet Tatooine.

Enter STORMTROOPERS 3 *and* 4.

TROOPER 3   There was someone within this pod, indeed.
              The tracks go off in this direction. See?
TROOPER 4   Behold, Sir, either someone large hath dropp'd
              His ring, or else this fragile circle here
              Doth mean we have found droids on Tatooine!   5
                                        [Exeunt stormtroopers.

Enter JAWAS *with* DROIDS, *including* C-3PO *and* R2-D2.

C-3PO	At last this vehicle of death hath stopp'd!
	So greatly fear I what shall happen next
	That I am shaken to my core within.
	They say that fear is better fac'd when two
	Together stand. Thus, swift shall I awake 10
	My dear R2. Wake up, wake up!
R2-D2	—Beep, squeak!
C-3PO	We're doomed! Dost thou think they shall melt
	us down?
JAWA 1	Me punna tynda ding. Utinni! Beh!
C-3PO	Shoot not! O shall this torment never end?
	First captur'd by these Jawas small and vile, 15
	And now we face a fate that is unknown.
	Now seems the first fate better than the next—
	Aye, rather would I bear the ill I have,
	Than fly to others that I know not of.

Enter OWEN LARS *and* LUKE SKYWALKER, *with* BERU LARS
aside in Lars homestead.

OWEN	Anon, now let us go!
BERU	—O Luke! O Luke! 20
	Pray, tell thine uncle that if he should find
	A translator, be sure it Bocce speaks.
	[*Aside:*] 'Tis true, the last time Owen bought a droid,
	More dud than droid we purchas'd in the deal.
LUKE	It seemeth we have little choice, dear aunt. 25
	And yet shall I remind him what thou say'st.
	[*Exit Beru into Lars homestead.*
OWEN	Again it falls to me, a simple man,

To take a leading role in matters grave.
For I must choose a droid today, 'tis true,
But also must I teach this lad, this Luke,   30
To learn and grow, and to become a man.
Although when I was young I too had dreams
Of far-off stars and distant galaxies,
I learn'd to work the land, to raise the crops.
And thus shall I my trade pass on to him,   35
Adopted son of mine and strangely dear.
I had not ask'd for Fate to bring a son
To me, for I had thought to have no heir.
Yet do Beru and I feel for this child
A measure of affection, and—as well—   40
The burden of responsibility.
[*To Jawa 2:*] Pray tell me, Jawa small,

                            what hast today?

JAWA 2   Me punna tynda ding.

OWEN   —Nay, not that one.
[*Aside:*] These Jawas offer first the lowliest,
'Tis ever in their nature to deceive.   45
[*To C-3PO:*] Droid, I assume that thou art

                        programmed well
For etiquette and protocol. 'Tis true?

C-3PO   Aye, protocol—my prim'ry function 'tis!
I am well versed in all the customs, Sir.

OWEN   No need have I of droids with protocol.   50

C-3PO   Not in this habitat, thou speakest true:
Hath ever sand a need of protocol?
When did a stone or rock need etiquette?
However, I am also made—

OWEN   —Peace! What
I need's a droid who knows the bin'ry tongue   55
Of moisture vaporators.

C-3PO   —O, but Sir!
My first employment was in programming
A bin'ry load a'lifter very like
Thy vaporators. Aye, in most respects.
[*Aside:*] My service and my worth I'll prove to him   60
If I must speak a thousand hours more.
For certain, I shall die ere I return
Once more to be in rank captivity.

OWEN Well. Speak'st thou Bocce?

C-3PO   —Truly Sir! 'Tis like
A second tongue unto my soul.

OWEN   —Pray, cease!   65
[*To Jawas:*] So shall I have this one here.

C-3PO   [*Aside:*]—Praise the day!
Now if he chooseth also my R2,
Aye, then shall I be pleas'd.

JAWA 1   —Mabbin beh!

OWEN   —Luke!
Take thou these droids unto our vast garage.
My wish it is they clean'd be ere we dine.   70

LUKE But unto Tosche Station would I go,
And there obtain some pow'r converters. Fie!

OWEN Thou canst go with thy friends another time,
When all thy chores have been fulfilled. Go to!

LUKE [*aside:*] O how shall I be mock'd, and verily   75
Abusèd when my noble comrades hear
That once again my uncle hath denied

My fervent wish to be with them instead.
[*To Owen:*] 'Tis well. [*To Droids:*] Come hither! Thou
                              too, Red.

R5-D4   —Beep hoo.

LUKE   Go hence!

R2-D2   —Beep, squeak, beep, beep, squeak
                          meep beep, beep!   80

[*Aside:*] If I go not with him, my foolishness
Shall render no one service. Thus, I beep.

JAWA 2   Bwana beh!

R2-D2   —Ahh!

                  [*R5-D4 begins to smoke and fail.*

LUKE   —Pray, uncle Owen, look!
Behold! This R2 unit hath a foul
And smoking motivator!

OWEN   —Vicious knave!   85
Say, in what manner dost thou try upon
Our goodly wills to ply thy thievery?
So shall I rip thy brown and ragged robes
To shreds, if thou set not this matter right.
Now speak!

JAWA 1   —Me punna tynda ding.

R2-D2   —Beep, squeak!   90

C-3PO   [*to Luke:*] Your pardon, Sir. The R2 unit which
Thou seest is in prime condition, aye,
A bargain 'tis, and he shall serve thee well.
[*Aside:*] Now if I can convince the human here
To purchase R2 too, along with me,   95
So shall I win the day! And ever shall
Yon R2-D2 dwell in peace with me.

	What shall he answer?
LUKE	—Uncle Owen, say!
	Hast thou consider'd yonder blue droid there?
OWEN	What of that blue one? That one shall be ours. 100
C-3PO	[aside:] O vict'ry! Next, I'll praise him for his choice.
	[To Luke:] A noble choice thou makest, Master, for
	Thou surely shalt be pleas'd with this new droid.
	I can with confidence report to thee
	That he is in first-class condition, Sir, 105
	For I have work'd with him before. He comes!
R2-D2	Beep, meep, beep, squeak.
LUKE	—Anon, away we go.

[Exeunt Luke, Owen, Jawas, and Droids.

C-3PO	Forget thou not this moment, faithless droid!
	Why I should put my neck at risk for thee
	Is quite beyond my mind's capacity. 110

[Exeunt.

SCENE 6.

Inside the Lars homestead.

Enter LUKE SKYWALKER, C-3PO, *and* R2-D2.

C-3PO	All praise be to the Maker, verily,
	This oily bath much healing shall provide.
	The glow of bright Coruscant doth not match
	The vital warmth this soothing oil brings me.
	The case of dust contamination which 5
	Befalls me mighty is, and renders me

	Unable—I'll be sworn—to move at all!	
LUKE	I rue the day I came unto this place,	
	This drab and barren rock call'd Tatooine.	
	But wherefore have I reason to complain?	10
	Do sandstorms not invade both rich and poor?—	
	We are not promis'd equity in life.	
	Both rich and poor alike pertain to me:	
	For certain, though in toil am I most rich,	
	By want of keen adventure am I poor.	15
	Thus I declare that whether rich or poor,	
	The lot I have receiv'd from Fate's unfair!	
	My comrade Biggs hath rightly guess'd, I fear,	
	That never shall I leave this stricken place!	
C-3PO	[*aside:*] O exclamation tragic! Shall I speak?	20
	[*To Luke:*] Is there, dear Sir, aught I might do to help?	
LUKE	Nay, droid, 'less thou canst alter time, or make	
	The harvest come apace, or, goodly friend,	
	If thou canst somehow bear my body hence	
	By magical conveyance yet unknown.	25
C-3PO	I think not, Sir, for merely droid am I,	
	And have not knowledge of such things as thou.	
	Not on this planet, anyway. In troth,	
	I do not know which planet this one be.	
LUKE	If center bright the universe contains,	30
	Then surely, droid, hast thou now found thyself	
	As far from it as thou canst poss'bly be.	
C-3PO	I see, Sir.	
LUKE	—Surely, thou may'st call me Luke.	
C-3PO	I see, Sir Luke.	
LUKE	—Thou jolly droid, just Luke.	

| | [*Aside:*] This droid, I see, is wont to prattle on, | 35 |

[*Aside:*] This droid, I see, is wont to prattle on,   35
Belike his mouth is faster than his mind.
                   [*Luke begins to clean R2-D2.*

C-3PO   C-3PO am I, an expert in
The human-cyborg link. And he, my short
Blue counterpart, is R2-D2 called.

LUKE   Good e'en.

R2-D2   —Beep, squeak!

LUKE   —Thou hast much carbon here,   40
It seemeth much of Fortune thou hast known.
Aye, can it be that two such droids as you
Can know more of adventure than a man?

C-3PO   With all we have been through, amaz'd am I
We yet our good condition keep, what with   45
Rebellion and its hurly-burly ways.

LUKE   Nay, can it be? The very thing of which
I would know more thou hast experienc'd?
Pray, knowest thou of the rebellion 'gainst
The Empire, droid?

C-3PO   —For certain, aye, 'tis how   50
We came to be in thine employment, if
Thou comprehend my simple meaning, Sir.
[*Aside:*] Now is his visage turn'd all eagerness—
O never in this manner have I seen
A man intoxicated with a dream!   55

LUKE   And hast thou been in many battles? Speak!
Whatever morsel thou mayst serve to me
Shall be a feast unto my waiting ear;
The smallest tale of battle lost or won
Shall feed my soul's ne'er-ending appetite!   60

C-3PO   Full many battles, aye, Sir. But I fear
           I have but little food to fill thy heart—
           A banquet, sadly, I cannot prepare,
           'Tis certain that of tales I am no chef.
           But rather, I confess that not much more   65
           Than an interpreter am I, and not
           Much good at telling stories—verily,
           I've not the salt or spice to season them.

LUKE   'Tis well, my droid. So shall my hunger wait
           To feast one day upon another's tale.   70
           [To R2-D2:] My little 'bot, thou hast got
                                         something jamm'd
           Herein. Hast thou been on a cruiser or—

Enter PRINCESS LEIA, *in beam projected by* R2-D2.

LEIA   O help me, Obi-Wan Kenobi, help.
           Thou art mine only hope.

LUKE   —Pray, what is this?

R2-D2   Squeak?

C-3PO   —What is what? A question hath
                                         he asked!   75
           Say, what is that?

LEIA   —O help me, Obi-Wan
           Kenobi, help. Thou art mine only hope.
           O help me, Obi-Wan Kenobi, help.
           Thou art mine only hope.

R2-D2   —Beep, meep, meep, hoo.
           Squeak, beep, meep, beep.

C-3PO   —He says 'tis nothing, Sir.   80

	A mere malfunction, bygone data 'tis.
	Please, pay no mind.
LUKE	—But who is she? For she
	Is far more beautiful than all the stars.
C-3PO	I truly do not know, Sir. I suspect
	She was a passenger on our last trip,
	A person of importance, I believe.
	[*Aside:*] First 'twas adventure, second 'tis this lass.
	'Tis certain my new Master hath a wealth
	Of passion, ever eager to bestow.
LUKE	Say, is there any more recording, droid?
R2-D2	Squeak, beep!
C-3PO	—Behave thyself, R2! For thou
	Shalt get us both in trouble. Be content,
	And trust him true. He is our master now.

85

90

R2-D2   Beep, beep, beep, meep, beep, squeak, beep,
                                  meep, squeak, hoo.

C-3PO   He saith he doth belong to Obi-Wan   95
         Kenobi, resident of parts nearby,
         And 'tis a private message meant for him.
         For all my wit, I know not what he means,
         For our last Master Sir Antilles was.
         Alas, with all we have endur'd, this dear   100
         Small R2 unit quite eccentric is.

R2-D2   Squeak!

LUKE   —Obi-Wan Kenobi . . . I suspect
         Old Ben Kenobi he doth mean, perhaps.
         First droids, then tales of battles fought in space,
         And now a damsel cries in beams of light!   105
         Did ever destiny come knocking thus?

C-3PO   I beg thy pardon, Sir, but know'st thou aught
         Of what he speaks?

LUKE   —I know not any man
         Nam'd Obi-Wan Kenobi, yet old Ben
         Resides beyond the Dune Sea, and there dwells   110
         Much like a hermit, strange and lone.

LEIA   —O help
         Me, Obi-Wan Kenobi, help. Thou art
         Mine only hope.

LUKE   —I wonder who she is.
         Whoever she may be, whatever is
         Her cause, I shall unto her pleas respond.   115
         Not e'en were she my sister could I know
         A duty of more weight than I feel now.
         It seemeth she some dreadful trouble hath—

        Mayhap I should replay the message whole.

R2-D2   Beep, squeak, squeak! Meep, hoo, meep.

C-3PO   —R2 doth say   120

        The bolt restraining him short-circuited

        His full recording system. So saith he,

        That if thou wouldst with speed remove the bolt,

        He may the full recording then display.

        [*Aside:*] What purpose shall I serve unto this man?   125

        Am I to guide, encourage, counsel—what?

        Thus shall I play the wise interpreter,

        For truly 'tis the part I know the best.

LUKE   What? Aye, thou seem'st too small to run away

        If I should take this off. Good little droid,   130

        So cleverly thou bringest messages,

        That thou hast won my trust. Now, thou art free.

                      [Exit Princess Leia from beam.

        But wait, where hath she gone? What villainy!

        How hast thou dampen'd that celestial light

        Wherein she spoke of late? Now bring her back,   135

        Play back the message full, thou naughty droid!

R2-D2   Meep, meep?

C-3PO   —What message, errant droid? The one

        Thou hast been playing, which thou hold'st within

        Thy rusty innards. [*Aside:*] O, alas! We shall

        Deactivated be!

BERU   [*inside:*]   —O Luke? Pray, Luke?   140

LUKE   I shall be there anon, good aunt Beru!

C-3PO   I'm sorry, Sir. For it doth seem he hath

        Acquir'd a minor flutter.

LUKE   —Thus she comes,

And thus she goes. Yet ever on my sight
Her beautiful, fine countenance shall shine.   145
So here's my vow: I'll see her once again,
In beam, or—hope on hope!—with my own eyes.
For now, I must depart to dine. Pray, see
If thou canst remedy this R2, droid.

                                        [Exit Luke.

R2-D2   Hoo.
C-3PO   —Reconsider, thou, if thou shalt play   150
          The message back for him.
R2-D2   —Beep, meep, hoo, whee?
C-3PO   Nay, I do not believe he liketh thee.
R2-D2   Beep, squeak?
C-3PO   —Nay, thee I like not either.
R2-D2   —Hoo.

                                        [Exit C-3PO.

Now are the pieces all arrang'd for me
To make a daring move, and fly this place.   155
The fool who sets the game in motion shall
Appear unto C-3PO and Luke
No more than if he were an arrant knave.
But hear the voice of R2-D2, all:
My noble purpose I'll accomplish yet—   160
To take to Obi-Wan the princess' news,
To take my Master Luke away from here,
And, in the end, perhaps more vital still—
To make connection twixt the two good men.
A foolish thing this flight may seem to thee,   165
And yet more fine than foolish shall it be.

                                        [Exeunt.

SCENE 7.

Inside the Lars homestead.

Enter OWEN LARS, BERU LARS, *and* LUKE SKYWALKER, *eating at a table.*

LUKE   Mine uncle, thou shouldst know my mind. Methinks
       The R2 unit we have bought belike
       May have been stolen.

OWEN   —Thievery hath e'er
       Been part and parcel of the Jawas' trade.
       But in thine utterance I sense there's more,   5
       So say, young Luke, why thinkest thou thereon?

LUKE   Good uncle, well I know the Jawas' tricks,
       Yet, as thou sayest, I mean something more.
       A stolen moment with those droids hath shown
       To me a reason they may stolen be: 10
       I did uncover a recording whilst
       I clean'd the R2 unit. He purports
       To be the property of someone known
       As Obi-Wan Kenobi. Thus, thought I,
       That he may stolen be. As to the name,   15
       This Obi-Wan Kenobi, wondered I
       If mayhap he meant Ben. Canst thou make sense?

OWEN   Nay.

LUKE   —Yet I wonder if this Obi-Wan
       Perchance may be some kin to yonder Ben.

OWEN   [*aside:*] Fie, fie! Shall that old man now
               haunt my home? 20
       [*To Luke:*] That wizard is a damnèd scurvy man.

Tomorrow shalt thou take the R2 droid
To Anchorhead and have its memory
Eras'd. And so shall there an end be to't.
For it belongeth only now to us.   25

LUKE   Aye, yet what if this Obi-Wan appears
And lays his claim unto this R2 droid?
What's stolen may be worth the looking for.

OWEN   The looking shall not happen, nor the find,
For I believe the man doth not exist.   30
[*Aside:*] Now shall I by a lie destroy the man,
Lest he be giv'n new life in Luke's young mind—
The boy a keen imagination hath.
[*To Luke:*] This Obi-Wan hath not for ages walk'd
Within this universe: he is no more.   35
'Twas many moons ago the old man died,
Aye, truly he hath met his end about
The time so long ago when wars were fought,
The time when men did battle to the grave,
The time before the Empire rul'd supreme,   40
The time wherein thy father died as well.

LUKE   Knew he my father?

OWEN   [*aside:*]   —Though I tell of men
And wars and battles brave, still all he hears
Is that word "father." [*To Luke:*] Prithee, Luke, forget.
Thy task is to prepare the droids for work   45
Tomorrow. In the morning shall they be
Upon the south ridge, laboring with those
Condensers.

LUKE   —Aye, and I believe these droids
Shall serve us well. In troth, good uncle, now

I must confess my mind is mov'd to think   50
Upon the pact 'twixt thee and me, and our
Agreement, namely that I shall stay here
Another season. Crops that grow in these
Harsh climes will surely grow sans me. And so,
Mine uncle, if these droids will satisfy   55
I wish my application to transmit
Unto the great Academy this year.

OWEN   Nay Luke, an uncle's heart is breaking! Canst
Thou mean the next semester hence, before
The harvest-time?

LUKE   —Just so! Quite plentiful   60
Are droids!

OWEN   —But harvest-time I need thee most!
Wilt thou here in the desert yet desert?
'Tis only one more season. This year I
Shall make enough at harvest-time to hire
More hands to help. Then canst thou go next year   65
To the Academy. To pilot is
A noble trade, my boy, but family
Is nobler still. I prithee, understand,
I need thee, Luke.

LUKE   —'Tis one more year entire!

OWEN   'Tis only one more season!

LUKE   —Aye, so saidst   70
Thou when my dear friends Biggs and Tank did leave.
Now cracks a hopeful heart, when, by the land,
A man's ambitions firmly grounded are:
So shall a bird ne'er learn to fly or soar
When wings are clipp'd by crops and roots and soil.   75

BERU   Pray whither fly'st thou, Luke?

LUKE   —It seems, dear aunt,
              I nowhere go nor flee nor sail nor fly.
              Instead, I must remain and clean those droids.

                                        [Exit Luke.

BERU   O Owen, he cannot abide for aye
              With us. 'Tis true, his friends are mostly gone.   80
              It hath great meaning for our well-lov'd Luke—
              This bird would surely fly.

OWEN   —So promise I
              That I shall set all things aright, Beru.
              The bird shall fly indeed, when time is ripe,
              And when the nest hath no more need of him.   85

BERU   But Owen, he hath not a farmer's heart—
              This apple falls quite near his father's tree.

OWEN   'Tis true! And this, my dear, is what I fear.

              *[Exeunt Owen and Beru. Reenter Luke, gazing into
                          the setting of Tatooine's two suns.*

LUKE   O, I am Fortune's fool. 'Tis true, 'tis true,
              And gazing now upon the double sun   90
              Of my home Tatooine, I know full well
              That elsewhere lies my destiny, not here.
              Although my uncle's will is that I stay,
              My heart within me bursts to think on it
              For out among the spheres I wish to roam—   95
              Adventure and rebellion stir my blood.
              Those oft-repeated words of my mate Biggs
              I do believe—that all the world's a star.
              Beyond that heav'nly light I shall fly far!

                                        [Exit.

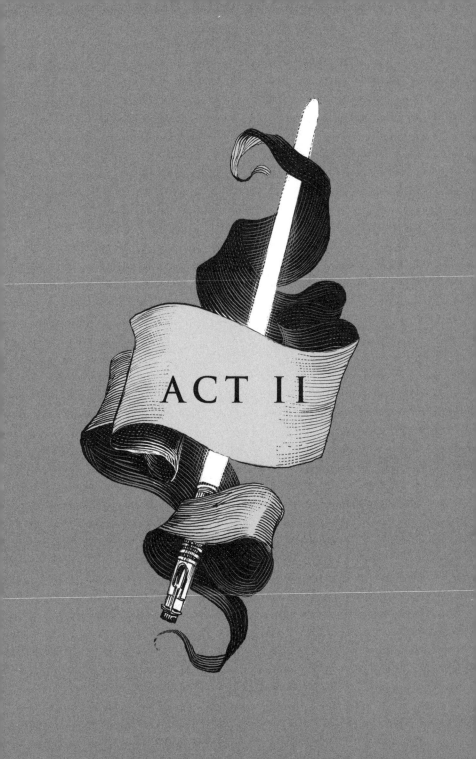

ACT II

SCENE 1.

Inside the Lars homestead.

Enter C-3PO.

C-3PO   Alas! My R2-D2, he hath flown,
And all the while he beepeth on and on
About his duty in rebellion's cause.
O with what strength shall I be punishèd
When R2's treachery discover'd is!   5
So shall I hide myself behind this ship
In hopes I'll not be found by Master Luke.
                                [C-3PO hides.

Enter LUKE SKYWALKER.

LUKE   C-3PO, I say, what dost thou there?
At what game playest thou, O jolly droid?
                           [C-3PO emerges.

C-3PO   I prithee, Sir, be thou not cross with me.   10
'Twas through no fault of mine, in truth I swear!
Pray let me not deactivated be.
I ask'd him, aye, and urg'd him not to go.
With sighs and words aplenty plied I him—
With many earnest pleadings made my cause—   15
And yet he was to me as one made deaf.
His metal ears, as 'twere, did seem to plug,
As though no word of mine could penetrate
And break upon his sense of hearing. O!

	I fear a curs'd malfunction doth befall	20
	My dear and treasur'd R2 unit.	
LUKE	—Nay!	
C-3PO	Aye, verily! His mission is supreme,	
	So sayeth he. He will not hinder'd be,	
	Nor from his wayward, stubborn purpose veer.	
CHORUS	Now with these words young Luke doth quickly run	25
	Beyond the shutter'd doors, with failing hope.	
	And stepping out beneath the setting sun	
	He scans the vast horizon with his scope.	
C-3PO	Sir, ever hath that R2 unit been	
	A problem that hath vex'd me through and through.	30
	Astromech droids have ever puzzl'd me:	
	Their minds have tempers mighty to behold,	
	Though all contain'd in frames of modest size.	
LUKE	Fie! How have I so easily been trick'd?	
	This R2 hath perform'd his greatest feat:	35
	To vanish—scope to wheels—into the air!	
	O blast it! Aye, and fie and ficos too!	
C-3PO	[aside:] Now he is anger'd. Peace, my Master, peace!	
	[To Luke:] Good Sir, forgive my impudence, but may	
	We yet this e'en go out asearching?	
LUKE	—Nay.	40
	'Tis far too dangerous. The night is dark,	
	But darker are the dreaded Sand People,	
	And darkest most of all their thievery.	
	Thus, as the darkness waits for light to dawn,	
	So must we wait for morning to arrive.	45
OWEN	[inside:] O Luke, come hither! Swiftly come ye in!	
	The time hath come to darken down the pow'r.	

LUKE   Anon, good uncle! Thy good word I'll heed!
               [*To C-3PO:*] O, I shall taste the whips and scorns of my
               Dear uncle's anger. So shall that small droid,   50
               Though yet far gone, wreak havoc on my soul.

C-3PO   Aye, Sir, 'tis true. Although the droid is skill'd
               At laboring and service, most doth he
               Excel at wearying the hearts of men.

                    [*Luke and C-3PO withdraw for the night.*

CHORUS   And so a restless night doth pass within: 55
               While Luke doth ponder future punishment
               And longs for his lost droid search to begin,
               C-3PO doth fear his banishment.
               At early morn, with eager wills they rise,
               A shar'd endeavor binding them anew.   60
               The fast landspeeder o'er the desert flies—
               They go to find the errant droid R2.

          LUKE *and* C-3PO *enter, flying in landspeeder.*

LUKE   Good friend, take heed! The scanner doth report
               A droid ahead. Pray, swiftly take us hence—
               Belike our R2-D2 there awaits!   65
               [*Aside:*] Perhaps I'll yet escape my uncle's wrath.

CHORUS   While droid and man go racing 'cross the sand,
               The Tusken Raiders watch the two pass by.
               Their banthas mounting, gaffi sticks at hand,
               They heave unto the air their warring cry.   70

                    Enter R2-D2.

         [Luke and C-3PO dismount to speak to R2-D2.

LUKE   Pray, whither goest thou, thou naughty droid?

R2-D2   Beep, meep, beep squeak.

C-3PO   —Nay, Master Luke is now
        Thy rightful owner. Learn obedience!
        Aye, learn thou loyalty! Pray, learn respect!
        And learn thou not to speak of Obi-Wan   75
        Kenobi!

R2-D2   —Whee, nee, squeak.

C-3PO   —Speak not to me
        Of mission, droid! I'll warrant, happy thou
        Shalt be if our new Master doth not let
        Thee know the blaster's deadly touch today.

LUKE   Pray, patience, dear C-3PO, 'tis well.   80
        But let us hence.

R2-D2   —Beep, whistle, nee, meep, squeak!

LUKE   What can the matter be? What doth he say?

C-3PO   He doth report that creatures hither come,
        Approaching stealthily from the southeast.

LUKE   Sand People! Hither, come, and let us see!   85
        [Aside:] Unbidden doth adventure come, yet here
        I stand, prepar'd to rise and welcome Fate.
        The twisting strand she threads we must but trail,
        For 'tis the wire that leadeth us through life.
        Fate's hand hath plac'd me here on Tatooine   90
        And now she beckons onward to th'abyss.
        Now o'er adventure's great abyss I perch—
        Above all time, above the universe,
        Above the rim of chance and destiny—
        And sister Fate doth dare me to look in.   95

And there—aye there!— I find my happiness.
I peer therein, embrace my Fate—and blink.
Come, life! For I am ready now to live.
[*With scope, to droids:*] I spy two banthas,
                     yet no Sand People.
Wait, wait, one doth appear unto me now—   100

CHORUS   With sudden viciousness the Tuskens come,
They knock young Luke and cause the droid to fall.
They seek to take a harshly pillag'd sum,
Till frighten'd by a false krayt dragon call.

Enter OBI-WAN KENOBI, *who has made a krayt dragon call to
frighten off the Tusken Raiders.*

OBI-WAN   Now enter I the scene of this boy's life: 105
             This boy whom I have watch'd for many years
             Hath grown into the man before me now.
             My hope I now entrust to him alone,
             That he might be our sure deliverance.
             And yet, this situation warrants care—   110
             I must approach with caution as we speak,
             And meet his questions as a trusted guide.
             My inner joy I must with patience hide,
             For certain 'tis it gives me great delight
             To see him now—his face, his golden hair!   115
             So long have I watch'd o'er him from afar,
             So many hours and days of my life spent
             In hopeful expectation of this one.
             In his beginning I shall find my end;
             This business shall reveal my final stage.   120
             Yet in my closing scenes perhaps I'll write
             A worthy ending to my mortal days:
             'Tis possible that in this gentle one
             The dream I've long awaited shall come true.
             So I'll compose a final act that shall   125
             Accomplish two most worthy ends: to set
             The world aright and save this old man's soul.
             [*To R2-D2:*] Well met, my little one.
R2-D2   [*aside:*]   —Almost I could
             My metal tongue release and speak to him.
             This man doth show sure signs of wisdom and   130
             Experience. [*To Obi-Wan:*] Beep, beep, meep, beep,
                 meep, squeak.
OBI-WAN   Come hither, tiny friend, be not afraid.

R2-D2   Beep, squeak, whee, hoo.

OBI-WAN   —Nay, prithee fret thou not.
           For he shall make a full recovery.

                                        [*Luke wakes.*

           Rest easy, lad, for thou hast had a fall—   135
           And more adventure hast thou seen today
           Than many in a lifetime do. I say,
           Thou catchest Fortune's favor to survive
           A cruel attack from Sand People most vile.

LUKE   But, by this light! 'Tis Ben Kenobi here!   140
           It fills my heart with joy and soothes my pain
           To meet thee.

OBI-WAN   —Aye, 'tis well. But let's go hence.
           The Jundland Wastes no place for trav'lers is.
           Now prithee, good young Luke, say wherefore art
           Thou here, and what strange errand bringeth thee   145
           Herein where I am wont to dwell?

LUKE   —This droid.
           Aye, truly, he hath brought me here.

R2-D2   —Beep, meep.

LUKE   It seemeth unto me that he doth search
           To find his former master, yet in all
           My days I ne'er have such devotion seen—   150
           As this one showeth—from a droid.

R2-D2   —Hoo.

LUKE   —Yet
           He claims that he belongeth to a man
           Nam'd Obi-Wan Kenobi, and I thought,
           Perchance, the man some relative of yours
           May be. Dost thou know any by such name?   155

OBI-WAN [*aside:*] O how the heart inside me breaks to hear
That name I once was call'd so long ago—
But happy Fate that 'tis Luke's voice that calls!
[*To Luke:*] Aye, Obi-Wan Kenobi, Obi-Wan
Kenobi. [*Aside:*] O, the name is like a song— 160
Yet whether glorious song of joy or else
Some dirge of bitter pain I'm yet unsure.
[*To Luke:*] It is a name I have not heard for lo
These many, many years—a long, long time.

LUKE My uncle knoweth Obi-Wan, I ken. 165
He doth report to me the man is dead.

OBI-WAN [*aside:*] O Owen, wretched knave! Such base deceit,
And yet I know full well why thou so spok'st.
Should I have acted diff'rent in thy place?
[*To Luke:*] But nay, the man takes not
his final sleep. 170
At least—unto this moment now—not yet.

LUKE Then know'st thou him?

OBI-WAN —Aye, verily I do.
I know the man as if he were myself,
For truly, aye, he is. This Obi-Wan,
Dear Luke, 'tis I.

R2-D2 [*aside:*] —By heaven's light! [*To Obi-Wan:*]
Beep, meep. 175

OBI-WAN I have not heard this name, this Obi-Wan,
Since ere e'en thou, thyself, wert born.

LUKE —Aye, then,
I see this little droid is bound to thee.

OBI-WAN I have no memory of owning such
A droid as this. 'Tis curious indeed. 180

[*Sound of Tusken Raiders aside.*] Now mark thee these
    my words: we must repair
Indoors to 'scape a second cudg'ling here.
The Sand People do easily take flight,
But soon they shall return with many more.

R2-D2   Beep, meep, beep, beep, meep, squeak!

LUKE   —C-3PO!   185
                [*C-3PO wakes, broken in pieces.*

C-3PO   Where am I? Have I ta'en an ill-tim'd step?
In dreams have I seen visions of my death—
Ten thousand soldiers pranc'd upon my grave,
And I, alone to face the murd'rous mass,
Could only weep at my untimely end.   190

LUKE   Peace, peace, good droid. Thou art alive, fear not.
Canst thou now stand? We quickly must depart
Before the Sand People attack us here
And strive to make thy dream reality.

C-3PO   O whether dream or waking, I know not,   195
But go thee hence, and save thyself, I pray.
C-3PO by nightmare hath been slain!

OBI-WAN   [*aside:*] This droid shall quickly stretch his welcome
                                     thin.

LUKE   I shall not leave thee, droid, thou speak'st sans sense.
Come, come, I'll bear thee up, so argue not.   200

OBI-WAN   [*aside:*] What noble care he takes to soothe this droid.
[*To Luke:*] We must make haste or face them yet again,
So hence let us away unto my den.
                                [*Exeunt.*

SCENE 2.

Inside the Kenobi homestead.

Enter Obi-Wan Kenobi, Luke Skywalker, C-3PO, *and* R2-D2.

LUKE   Nay, thou art sure misled, O wise one, for
                My father hath not fought in any wars.
                Full many evenings as I lay abed
                Such tales I heard of him I never knew:
                A navigator on a freighter ship   5
                Which carried fragrant spices hence to yon
                My father was. He kneweth naught of wars.
OBI-WAN   So hath thine uncle told thee. Marry, he
                Did not agree with aught thy father told
                Of his philosophy and brave ideals.   10
                Thine uncle, tether'd to the land, did not
                Believe thy father should become involv'd
                In matters of the stars and Empires, nay.
                [*Aside:*] What shall I of the father tell the child?
                If gentle Luke knew all that's known to me   15
                I'll warrant he'd not understand the rhyme
                And reason for my words. And yet, what is't
                To lie? To tell the truth, all else be damn'd?
                Or else to tell, perhaps, a greater truth?
                Is it the truth to tell a boy each fact   20
                And thus deface his father's memory?
                Or have I spoken better truth to Luke
                When I about his father speak with pride?

Aye, ev'ry child deserves a champion.

LUKE Hast thou done battle in the Clone Wars?

OBI-WAN   —Aye.   25
And once was I a Jedi Knight, the same
As thy dear father.

LUKE   —O, how tears well up
Within me for the loss of that dear man
Whom never I did know, nor do, nor will.

OBI-WAN I tell thee truly, 'mongst the pilots he   30
Was e'er the greatest in the galaxy.
He also was a cunning warrior,
And to the last was he a dear, dear friend.
[*Aside:*] And now to play upon his natur'l sense
Of self-importance, so to draw him near   35
To thoughts of Jedi training for himself.
[*To Luke:*] I hear thou art a pilot skill'd as well.
This calleth to my mind a gift I have
For thee. Thy father hath desir'd that thou
Shouldst have this weapon when thou wert of age. 40
Thine uncle, though, would none of it, so fear'd
He that thou might adjoin with Obi-Wan
Upon a fool's crusade or devil's task
Just as thy father hath when he was young.

C-3PO Dear Sir, if thou dost need me not, I shall   45
Shut down upon the present moment, here.

OBI-WAN [*aside:*] Why speak'st he here when 'tis my time
                                              to speak?
These droids of protocol are e'er uncouth:
Of etiquette they know but little, troth!

LUKE Pray tell, what is't?

OBI-WAN   —Thy father's lightsaber.   50
It is the weapon of a Jedi Knight:
If thou in thine own hand could hold a sun,
Then thou wouldst know the power of this tool.
Not merely random, neither awkward like
A blaster. Nay, the lightsaber maintains   55
A noble elegance, a Jedi's pride.
'Tis something for a civiliz'd new age.

CHORUS   Now holdeth Luke the weapon in his hand,
And with a switch the flame explodes in blue.
The noble light Luke's rev'rence doth command: 60
That instant was a Jedi born anew.

OBI-WAN   [aside:] Now doth the Force begin to work in him.
[To Luke:] For many generations Jedi were
The guarantors of justice, peace, and good
Within the Old Republic. Ere the dark   65
Times came and ere the Empire 'gan to reign.

LUKE   How hath my father died?

OBI-WAN   [aside:]   —O question apt!
The story whole I'll not reveal to him,
Yet may he one day understand my drift:
That from a certain point of view it may   70
Be said my answer is the honest truth.
[To Luke:] A Jedi nam'd Darth Vader—aye, a lad
Whom I had taught until he evil turn'd—
Did help the Empire hunt and then destroy
The Jedi. [Aside:] Now, the hardest words of all   75
I'll utter here unto this innocent,
With hope that one day he shall comprehend.
[To Luke:] He hath thy Father murder'd and betray'd,

And now are Jedi nearly all extinct.
Young Vader was seduc'd and taken by   80
The dark side of the Force.

LUKE   —The Force?

OBI-WAN   —The Force.
The Force doth give a Jedi all his pow'r,
And 'tis a field of energy that doth
Surround and penetrate and bind all things
Together, here within our galaxy.   85

R2-D2   [*aside:*] In hearing this wise man I have almost
My errand quite forgot. Now to my work!
[*To Obi-Wan:*] Beep, meep, meep, squeak, beep, whee,
                        squeak, whistle, meep!

OBI-WAN   And now, my little friend, shall I attempt
To find out whence thou came, and to discern   90
The reason wherefore thou hast left thy home
For lands unknown, a mission to pursue.

LUKE   He hath a message play'd—

OBI-WAN   —Thus have I found.

Enter PRINCESS LEIA, *in beam projected by* R2-D2.

LEIA   Dear General Kenobi, many years
Ago thou serv'd my noble father in   95
The Clone Wars. Now, he beggeth thee to come
Again and aid him in his struggle with
The Empire. Sadly may I not be there
With thee in person, my request to give.
My ship of late hath fallen under siege   100
And thus my mission—bringing thee unto

My cherish'd planet Alderaan—hath fail'd.
Yet have I deep within the mem'ry banks
Of this brave R2 unit stor'd the plans
Most vital for rebellion's victory.   105
My father can retrieve the plans therein,
But I must ask of thee to take the droid
And bring him unto Alderaan with care.
The desp'rate hour is now upon us—please,
I beg thee, Sir. O help me, Obi-Wan   110
Kenobi, help. Thou art mine only hope.

                     [Exit Princess Leia from beam.

CHORUS   The message ends, then doth a silence fall.
While Obi-Wan his duty contemplates,
Young Luke considers whether Fate doth call.
Aye—in this moment, destiny awaits.   115

OBI-WAN   [*aside:*] The boy doth hear and hath the taste of fire
New burning in his ears. Now shall I play
The part of fuel and gently stoke that fire.
[*To Luke:*] Thou must be taught the Force if thou
                              wouldst come
Away with me, and go to Alderaan.   120

LUKE   Nay, Alderaan? [*Aside:*] This man hath many charms,
And now it seems to me that I have been
These many hours under some great spell
That he hath cast. [*To Obi-Wan:*] Nay, I must hence
                                  back home.
'Tis late, and Uncle Owen shall be vex'd,   125
If I do not return to him ere long.

OBI-WAN   [*aside:*] And now it must be done or else 'tis lost!
[*To Luke:*] I need all thy good help, Luke—so doth she.

	For such adventures I have grown too old.
LUKE	Nay, nay, I should not be involv'd, dear friend. 130
	Much work there is to be completed yet,
	And as the seers say true, a crop without
	Its harvester is like a dewback sans
	Its rider. Verily, I loathe the cruel
	And noisome Empire, aye, yet nothing 'gainst 135
	It have I pow'r to do at present. Fie!
	'Tis all so far, far distant from this place.
OBI-WAN	Thus speaks thine uncle through thy lips, not thee.
LUKE	Mine uncle, O, mine uncle! How shall I
	To him explain this matter? Tell me, how? 140
OBI-WAN	Come now with me and learn the Force, dear Luke.
LUKE	[*aside:*] Now am I split in twain by Fate's sharp turns.
	Two paths: the one toward adventure leads,
	The other taketh me back to my home.
	I have, for all my life, long'd to go hence 145
	And now this Obi-Wan hath reason giv'n
	Why I should leave my Tatooine and fly
	Unto the stars. Aye, he hath told me of
	The pow'rful Force. And yet, another force
	Doth pull me home: the force of duty and 150
	Responsibility. I would go hence,
	Would fly today and ne'er look back again,
	Except Beru and Owen are my true
	And loyal family. 'Tis settled, then,
	I stay on Tatooine until the time 155
	When I may leave with clear, unfetter'd soul.
	[*To Obi-Wan:*] I shall take thee as far as Anchorhead.
	From there may'st thou find transport to where'er

Thou goest—aye, throughout the galaxy.

OBI-WAN   Thou must hold with thy conscience, it is true,   160
Whate'er thou thinkest right, thus thou shouldst do.

                                        [*Exeunt.*

SCENE 3.
Inside the Death Star.

Enter Imperial generals and Senators, including ADMIRAL MOTTI *and* COMMANDER TAGGE.

TAGGE   Until this battle station utterly
Prepar'd and operational shall be,
'Tis plainly vulner'ble to an attack.
The rebels have more resources and are
More dangerous that thou wilt deign to see.   5

MOTTI   Perhaps of danger to thy star fleet, aye,
But not unto this battle station strong.

TAGGE   Rebellion shall gain more support within
Th'Imperial Senate—

Enter GRAND MOFF TARKIN *and* DARTH VADER.

TARKIN   [*aside:*]   —O, these men do talk
And quibble like a brood of clucking hens!   10
[*To Tagge:*] Th'Imperial Senate, which thou speak'st
                                        of here,
No longer any threat to us doth hold.
For truly have I just receivèd word

	That our great Emperor himself dissolv'd	
	The Council—now the final remnants of	15
	The Old Republic fade away like dew.	
TAGGE	But marry, 'tis impossible! How shall	
	The Emperor maintain control without	
	The crimson cord of vast bureaucracy?	
VADER	[*aside:*] O, how these politicians irk me so!	20
	Of governors and territories care	
	I not! But I retain their company	
	For mine own purposes, and though their talk	
	Doth tire my mind I do confess that naught	
	I've found hath on their counsel yet improv'd.	25
	For ev'ry human bond is meaningless:	
	All family doth leave, and friends betray,	
	And lovers fail, and teachers turn, and thus	
	Among the politicians shall I dwell—	

Where lies, deceit, and garr'lous talk do make 30
The universe go 'round. But yet, I vow:
I'll not be govern'd by the governors,
No policy of politicians heed.
Instead, myself and my dear Emperor
Together shall pursue our destiny. 35

TARKIN The governors of all the regions now
Have sole control o'er their especial lands,
And fear shall keep the people all in line—
Fear of this very battle station, aye!

TAGGE But what, pray tell, of the Rebellion vile? 40
For if the rebels have the plans to this
Good station stolen, possible it is
They may have found a weakness, which, in haste,
They shall exploit. Pray, Tarkin, mark my words.

VADER Those plans shall soon recover'd be, fear not. 45

MOTTI Attack upon this station pointless is,
Regardless of the data they have found.
I speak not rashly when I here aver:
This station now hath power ultimate
O'er all else in the vast, wide universe! 50
And now, I prithee, let us see it us'd!

VADER [to Motti:] Nay, peace! I warn thee, man, be not
too proud
Of thy great terror technological.
A weapon for the mass destruction of
A planet—even to destroy it whole— 55
Is no match for the power of the Force.

MOTTI Thou shalt not 'tempt to frighten us with words
So like a man of magic, Vader. Nay,

        Thy sorc'rer's act is tir'd and overdone.

        The sad religion thou dost cling to hath   60

        No pow'r to conjure up the stolen plans.

        Nor dost thou have a third-eye's sight to make—

            [Vader begins to choke Motti using the Force.

CHORUS   The power of the Force is now unveil'd

        As Vader holds the Admiral in check.

        The Force that Motti with his words impal'd   65

        Now hath a wampa's hold about his neck.

VADER   I find thy lack of faith disturbing.

TARKIN   —Cease!

        No more of this! Good Vader, let him be.

VADER   As is thy will. *[Aside:]* My point hath well been made

        Upon his prideful, unbelieving throat.   70

                [Vader releases Motti.

TARKIN　　Enough! This endless bickering shall end.
　　　　　Lord Vader shall provide the setting of
　　　　　The errant rebel base before the time
　　　　　This station shall be operational.
　　　　　And then, my friends, the Empire shall rejoice—　　75
　　　　　Rebellion shall be crush'd in one swift stroke!
　　　　　Now get ye gone, fulfill this purpose grand.
　　　　　　　[Exeunt Imperial generals and Senators, including
　　　　　　　　　　Admiral Motti and Commander Tagge.

VADER　　My troopers on the planet Tatooine
　　　　　Have trac'd the creatures who have found the droids.
　　　　　We shall retrieve those plans.

TARKIN　　　　　　—'Tis well, 'tis well.　　80
　　　　　Thou ever wert a faithful servant to
　　　　　The Emperor, Lord Vader. Prithee, go,
　　　　　And take with thee a gov'nor's gratitude.
　　　　　　　　　　　　　[Exit Darth Vader.
　　　　　There goes a man who hath a mind to serve.
　　　　　The Emperor doth hold him in his grasp,　　85
　　　　　And lays a claim upon his heart and soul.
　　　　　Well I recall when, as a younger man,
　　　　　The Emperor and Vader with me stood
　　　　　And contemplated our shar'd destiny.
　　　　　Now Vader, split 'twixt manhood and machine,　　90
　　　　　Fulfills a vital place within my plans.
　　　　　Aye, though I fear the Force, he knows his place.
　　　　　He knoweth he and I stand side by side—
　　　　　Together wrapp'd in power's warm embrace—
　　　　　Our Emperor to serve until, at last,　　95
　　　　　The final curtain of life's play is dropp'd.

As history hath made this Tarkin great,
This battle station now shall make me fear'd.
I am as constant as the Endor moon,
And shall rebellion crush, and do it soon.   100

> *[Exit Grand Moff Tarkin.*

SCENE 4.
The desert planet Tatooine.

Enter OBI-WAN KENOBI, LUKE SKYWALKER, C-3PO, *and* R2-D2,
surrounded by Jawa corpses.

LUKE   It seemeth that the Sand People have done
              This wretched deed—yon gaffi sticks and tracks
              Of bantha, aye. But ne'er in all my years
              Have Tuskens gone awry so far as this.

OBI-WAN   And they have not, though they who this vile deed   5
              Have done, would make us think Sand People did.
              But hark! Take note, and look ye thereupon:
              Yon tracks are side by side, yet Sand People,
              'Tis known, e'er one behind the other ride,
              So better may they hide their numbers large.   10

LUKE   These Jawas are the very same who sold
              C-3PO—and R2-D2, too—
              Unto mine uncle not two days ago.

OBI-WAN   And these marks here, these blast points, are too fine
              And accurate for Sand People, 'tis true.   15
              For only stormtroopers by Empire train'd
              Are so precise and cunning in their work.

[*Aside:*] Survey'ng this scene, I fear what cometh next,
For certain have the troops more evil done.
Good Owen and Beru no doubt are slain,   20
And though it breaks my heart to think on it,
It may be that their deaths will spark Luke's soul,
And lead him unto good rebellion's cause.
So by their death may others yet find life.

LUKE   But why, say why, would these Imperi'l troops   25
Have aught to do with Jawas? Wait, I see—
The droids! If they have trac'd them here they may
Have soon discover'd whom they sold them to,
Which—O, my soul!—would lead them to my home!

OBI-WAN   Pray, patience, Luke! 'Tis far too dangerous!   30

[*Luke runs to his landspeeder.*

CHORUS   Now flies Luke off in his landspeeder quick
And finds his home engulf'd in flames of red,
Then spies amid the smoke, so black and thick,
The bodies of his aunt and uncle, dead.
A sadder, wiser man he cometh back,   35
With noble purpose now his life's imbu'd.
By wrongful, vicious, cowardly attack,
The Empire hath Luke's passion quite renew'd.

OBI-WAN   'Twas nothing thou, Luke, couldst have done
had thou
Been there. Thou murder'd would have been as well.   40
Aye, also would the droids now captur'd be
And would be in the Empire's evil hands.

LUKE   Thou knowest, friend, what I have seen today.
No sorrow like to this have I e'er known.
I wish to come with thee to Alderaan,   45

For nothing have I here on Tatooine.
Then shall I learn the Force, and shall become
A Jedi like my father. Thus I vow.
So let's prepare and go upon our way,
With haste may we escape the troopers vile.   50
        [Exeunt Obi-Wan, C-3PO, and R2-D2.
Adventure have I ask'd for in this life,
And now have I too much of my desire.
My soul within me weeps; my mind, it runs
Unto a thousand thousand varied paths.
My uncle Owen and my aunt Beru,   55
Have they been cruelly kill'd for what I want?
So shall I never want again if in
The wanting all I love shall be destroy'd.
O fie! Thou knave adventure! Evil trick
Of boyhood's mind that ever should one seek   60
To have adventure when one hath a home—
A family so kind and full of love,
Good, steady work, and vast, abundant crops—
Why would one give up all this gentle life

For that one beastly word: adventure? Fie!   65
But soft, my soul, be patient and be wise.
The sands of time ne'er turnèd backward yet,
And forward marches Fate, not the reverse.
So while I cannot wish for them to live,
I can my life commit unto their peace.   70
Thus shall I undertake to do them proud
And take whate'er adventure comes my way.
'Tis now my burden, so I'll wear it well,
And to the great Rebellion give my life.
A Jedi shall I be, in all things brave—   75
And thus shall they be honor'd in their grave.

                                        [Exit Luke.

ACT III

SCENE 1.

Mos Eisley, on the desert planet Tatooine.

CHORUS   Now, in her cell the princess doth remain,
                With hope and trouble written on her face.
                At times she faces torture, horrid pain.
                With these tools Vader seeks the rebel base.
                While Leia in her captive state is kept,   5
                Young Luke and Obi-Wan set on their way.
                Approaching town, they hope to intercept
                A pilot to transport them sans delay.

                Enter OBI-WAN KENOBI, LUKE SKYWALKER, C-3PO,
                    and R2-D2, *riding in landspeeder.*

OBI-WAN   Mos Eisley spaceport. Never shalt thou find
                A hive more rank and wretched, aye, and fill'd   10
                With villainy. So must we cautious be.

                Enter STORMTROOPERS.

TROOPER 3   I prithee, speak, how long hast thou these droids?
LUKE   'Tis three or, mayhap, four full seasons now.
OBI-WAN   We are prepar'd to sell them, shouldst thou wish.
CHORUS   Now is the Force to noble purpose us'd—   15
                Not as the Sith, employing it to smite,
                Hath through the dark side rank the Force abus'd—
                Good Obi-Wan shall use the Force for right.
TROOPER 4   Pray, show me now thy papers.

OBI-WAN   —Nay, thou dost
                 Not need to see his papers.
TROOPER 4   —Nay, we do   20
                 Not need to see his papers.
OBI-WAN   —True it is,
                 That these are not the droids for which thou search'st.
TROOPER 3   Aye, these are not the droids for which we search.
OBI-WAN   And now, the lad may go his merry way.
TROOPER 3   Good lad, I prithee, go thy merry way!   25
OBI-WAN   Now get thee hence.
TROOPER 4   —Now get thee hence, go hence!
                                        [Exeunt stormtroopers.

Enter JAWAS as OBI-WAN KENOBI, LUKE SKYWALKER, C-3PO,
        and R2-D2 dismount landspeeder.

C-3PO   O, how those Jawas vex me!
LUKE   [to Jawas:]   —Get thee gone!
                                        [Exeunt Jawas.
                 Now by my troth, I cannot comprehend
                 How we those threat'ning stormtroopers did 'scape.
                 Aye, verily, I thought our end was nigh.   30
OBI-WAN   The Force hath mighty power o'er the weak
                 And simple-minded of this universe.
LUKE   Dost thou believe we shall therein, in yon
                 Dank place, discover any pilot who
                 Hath means to transport us to Alderaan?   35
OBI-WAN   A goodly crew of freighter pilots here
                 May oft be found. But prithee, take good care,
                 This small cantina hath an ill repute.

LUKE   I find myself prepar'd for ev'rything.

OBI-WAN   [*aside:*] The youth hath vigor—hopef'lly judgment,

                                            too.   40

                    [*They enter the cantina with many beings*
                                            and an innkeeper.

CHORUS   Now mark thee well, good viewer, what you see,

                 Such varied characters are on display!

                 For never hath there been such company

                 As in Mos Eisley gathers day by day.

                 The creatures gather 'round the central bar   45

                 While hammerheads and hornèd monsters talk,

                 A band compos'd of aliens bizarre:

                 This is the great cantina—thou may'st gawk!

INNKEEP.   [*to Luke:*] A word! Herein we shall not serve their

                                           kind—

                 Thy droids! They must depart beyond these walls.   50

LUKE   [*to droids:*] Good friends, pray wait beside the
                                                  speeder now,
              For we desire no conflict here today.
C-3PO   I do with all my heart agree, dear Sir.
                                          [*Exeunt droids.*

Enter CHEWBACCA, *speaking with* OBI-WAN *and two beings*
                     speaking to LUKE.

BEING 1   Negola d'waghi wooldugger!
BEING 2   —I say!
              He liketh not thy look.
LUKE   —Forgive me, Sir.   55
              [*Aside:*] Nor do I like his face, yet do I groan?
BEING 2   I do not like thy look. Indeed, young lad,
              I bite my thumb at thee. Proceed with care,
              For we two men are wanted by the law.
              Aye, I have earn'd the penalty of death   60
              In many systems, and would gladly earn
              It here as well, if thou provoke me to't.
LUKE   [*aside:*] I would, mayhap, be fearful if this man
              Hath even shoulder height on me attain'd.
              [*To Being 2:*] Tut, careful shall I be.
BEING 2   —Thou shalt be dead!   65
                                          [*Obi-Wan approaches.*
OBI-WAN   Pray, peace, this little lad's not worth thy time.
              Now come, let us be friends, my goodly Sir,
              Then shall we to thy health and welfare drink.
                                          [*Being 2 strikes Luke;*
                                          Obi-Wan brandishes his lightsaber,

             injuring Being 2 and severing Being 1's arm.
                          Exeunt Beings 1 and 2.

OBI-WAN   [*aside:*] I have no wish or purpose here to fight,
                Yet have these drunkards left me little choice.   70
                But there is yet a lesson to be learn'd:
                This Obi-Wan, though old, hath still the gift.
                [*To Luke:*] Chewbacca here doth service as first mate
                Upon a ship that may our purpose meet.

              Enter HAN SOLO, *who joins* CHEWBACCA,
                  OBI-WAN, *and* LUKE *at a table.*

HAN   Han Solo at thy service, gentlemen,   75
                The great *Millenn'um Falcon* is my ship.
                My first mate Chewie telleth me ye seek
                Safe passage to the system Alderaan.
OBI-WAN   Aye, true, if 'tis a vessel swift of flight.
HAN   "A vessel swift of flight," thou say'st? Hast thou   80
                Not heard of the *Millenn'um Falcon*, Sir?
OBI-WAN   [*aside:*] Now shall he boast. But if his ship we'd have,
                Some boasting we'll endure. [*To Han:*] Nay,
                                should I have?
HAN   'Tis but the ship that hath the Kessel run
                Accomplish'd in twelve parsecs, nothing more.   85
                Imperi'l starships have I slyly 'scap'd,
                But nothing more of that. And neither do
                I speak about bulk-cruisers small, but vast
                Corelli'n ships, yet nothing more, no more.
                I shall not brag about her speed, good Sir.   90
                Suffice to say the ship shall fill thy needs,

As she's the fastest e'er. But nothing more.

LUKE   [*aside:*] Aye, nothing more, I wish he'd hold his peace.
This man, it seems, doth love his ship far more
Than ere I saw a man his woman love.   95

HAN   Pray tell, what shall the cargo be?

OBI-WAN   —Myself,
The boy, two droids, and ne'er a question ask'd.

HAN   'Tis what, a touch of local trouble here?

OBI-WAN   Nay, let us simply say it thus: we would
Imperial entanglements avoid.   100

HAN   Aye, there's the rub, so shalt thou further pay.
Ten thousand is the cost, and ev'ry bit
Shalt thou deliver ere we leave the dock.

LUKE   Ten thousand? Fie! We could our own ship buy
For such a sum as this.

HAN   —A goodly jest!   105
For who should pilot such a ship—shouldst thou?

LUKE   Thou knave, I could indeed! A pilot skill'd
Am I in my own right. [*To Obi-Wan:*] Now should

                                    we stay,

And be abusèd more by this man's words?

OBI-WAN   Two thousand can we render to thee now,   110
And fifteen more deliver when we come
With safety unto Alderaan's bright port.

HAN   Say, seventeen? Congratulations, men,
Thou hast a ship secur'd, and we'll depart
Whene'er thou art prepar'd. Thou shalt find me   115
At docking harbor number ninety-four.

OBI-WAN   Aye, ninety-four.

HAN   —It seemeth that thou may

Already have provok'd some interest.

[Exeunt Obi-Wan and Luke as stormtroopers pass by.

CHEWBAC.   Egh.

HAN   —Seventeen! So must they desp'rate be!

This truly may my swift deliv'rance prove.   120
Go thou unto the ship and be prepar'd.

[Chewbacca exits.

In times now past have I poor judgments made,
And now these errors plague my very soul.
For freedom I was made—for taking wing!—
Yet as a markèd man I cannot fly.   125
For bound by debts, by duty and by fear,
I live my life along the razor's edge:
One part of me that hunts for better life,
And one part hunted for the life I've led.
My own existence is a paradox—   130
A smuggler with a lover's kindly heart,
A gambler with a noble spirit brave.
I would be better than it seems I am
If ever I transcend the man I was.
Perhaps this new employment shall reveal   135
The way I shall make straight my crooked path—
Thus heal my past and write a future new.

Enter GREEDO, *stopping* HAN SOLO *as the latter begins to exit.*

GREEDO   Na koona t'chuta, Solo?
HAN   —Yes, indeed,
Good Greedo, I have plann'd to make my way
Unto thy Master. Tell thou Jabba plain: 140

I have obtain'd his money.

GREEDO   —Soong peetch'lay.
Na mala tram pee chock makacheesa.
Na Jabba w'nin chee kosthpa murishan'
Tutyng ye wanya yoskah. Heh heh heh!
Na chas kee nyowyee koo chooskoo.

HAN   —'Tis true,   145
Yet this time is the money truly mine.

GREEDO   Keh lee chalya chulkah in ting coo'ng koos'.

HAN   [aside:] This bounty hunter doth my patience try.
[To Greedo:] Nay, nay, I have not money
                                        with me now.
Tell Jabba—

GREEDO   —Ny'chi withi! Ayl garu   150
Puyay enya aru gagu shuku
Shunu pu'aa ipi.

HAN   —But even I
From time to time have boarded been. Dost thou
Believe that e'er I had the choice?

GREEDO   —Dro Jabb'.
Na paknee abnya apna.

HAN   —Nay, not that: 155
The day when Jabba taketh my dear ship
Shall be the day you find me a grave man.

GREEDO   Nay oo'chlay nooma. Chespeka noofa
Na cringko kaynko, a nachoskanya!

HAN   Aye, true, I'll warrant thou hast wish'd this day.   160
            [They shoot, Greedo dies.
         [*To innkeeper:*] Pray, goodly Sir, forgive me for the
                         mess.
         [*Aside:*] And whether I shot first, I'll ne'er confess!
                       [Exeunt.

SCENE 2.

Inside the Death Star.

Enter DARTH VADER, GRAND MOFF TARKIN, *and*
COMMANDER TAGGE.

VADER   The princess hath shown great resistance to
         The mind probe—'twere as if she knew the Force
         And hath a Jedi's blood to overcome
         The piercing of her mind by a machine.
         Belike it shall some length of time yet be   5
         Until we can extract the thoughts therein.

Enter ADMIRAL MOTTI.

MOTTI   The final tests are now complete at last.
         And thus my news: the Death Star stands prepar'd.
         Aye, fully operational it is.
         So, Governor, what course shall we now set?   10
TARKIN   Perhaps the stubborn princess shall respond
         To an alternative persuasiveness.
VADER   I prithee, Tarkin, say: what dost thou mean?

TARKIN   Pray patience, Darth—thou shalt my meaning learn.

Now time it is the power of this Death   15

Star shown to all shall be. Now, Admiral,

Go forth and set thy course for Alderaan.

MOTTI   I understand thee, and with pride obey.

[Exeunt Grand Moff Tarkin, Commander Tagge,
and Admiral Motti.

VADER   The death of innocents doth bring me joy.

Because the dark side is my chosen path,   20

The senseless end of others pains me not.

For I have play'd the part of judge severe

And then have been the executioner.

Why would I care for those on Alderaan,

When I have murder'd innocents as they?   25

'Tis my dark calling, which I do embrace.

To Alderaan we fly on course direct,

And to this feast of death I'll not object.

[Exit Darth Vader.

SCENE 3.

Mos Eisley, on the desert planet Tatooine.

Enter C-3PO and R2-D2.

C-3PO   I prithee, lockest thou the door anon!

[They hide behind door.

Enter STORMTROOPERS.

TROOPER 5   This door is lock'd. And as my father oft
              Hath said, a lockèd door no mischief makes.
              So sure am I that, thus, behind this door
              Cannot be found the droids for which we search.   5
              And thus may we move on with conscience clear.
                   [Exeunt stormtroopers. C-3PO and R2-D2 emerge.

C-3PO   I'll tell thee true, I would with Master Luke
              Prefer to go than now remain with thee.
              I do not know what trouble here may be,
              Yet certain am I thou deserv'st the blame.   10

R2-D2   *[aside:]* I'll warrant, thou shalt have thy recompense!
              [To C-3PO:] Squeak, whistle, beep, meep, nee, meep,
                                        whistle, squeak!

C-3PO   Hold thou thy cursing and most cursèd tongue!

Enter OBI-WAN KENOBI *and* LUKE SKYWALKER.

OBI-WAN   Thou must thy speeder sell.
LUKE   —That matters not.
              For ne'er shall I return unto this place.   15
CHORUS   Young Luke doth with a buyer swiftly meet,
              And in a trice a hasty deal is wrought.
              A speeder sold along a dusty street—
              But with the sale new chance for hope is bought.
LUKE   A paltry sum, in truth! Aye, ever since   20
              The XP-38 hath been releas'd,
              This model hath but little value. Fie!
OBI-WAN   Fear not—it shall suffice. 'Twill serve our need.
                                        [All stand aside.
CHORUS   Now while young Luke and Obi-Wan prepare,

Their deeds are watch'd by eyes as yet unseen.   25
With black beak menacing he spies the pair,
Then comes another fiend with portly mien.

Enter HAN SOLO *with* CHEWBACCA *and* JABBA THE HUTT
with henchmen.

JABBA   Ba'Solo! Hay lapa no ya, Solo!
HAN   [*aside:*] Now, marry, 'tis an unexpected scene.
               [*To Jabba:*] Aye, here, thou Jabba slimy and rotund.   30
               I have awaited long thy coming here.
JABBA   Boonowa tweepi. Heh, ho, ha!
HAN   —Nay, nay!
               Thou didst not think that I should run, didst thou?
JABBA   Na-Han mah bukee. Keel-ee c'leya kuk'h.
               Wanta dah moolee-rah? Muh wonkee chee   35
               Sa crispo Greedo?
HAN   —Next time thou dost wish
               To counsel hold with me, pray come thyself!
               Send not thy churlish dismal-dreaming knaves.
JABBA   Han, Han. Make-cheesay. Pa'sa tah nay
               Ono caulky malia. Ee youngee   40
               D'emperiolo teesaw. Twa spastik'
               Wahl no. Yanee dah poo noo.
HAN   —Nay, see here!
               As I have said before—O verily,
               'Tis though I just have said thus—even I
               From time to time have boarded been. Dost thou   45
               Believe that e'er I had the choice? [*Aside:*] Aye, true,
               It sometimes seemeth I repeat myself.

[*To Jabba:*] Now have I, though, a simple charter
                          found,
      And soon as it is done, thy payment shall
      Be done as well—belike with interest.   50
      I need but time and I shall do it, Sir.
JABBA   Na-Han ma bukee. Bargon yanah cot'
      Da eetha. See fah luto tweentee, ee

    Yaba na—

HAN   —Nay, say thou not so much.

    Fifteen percent, I'll warrant, shall be well.   55

JABBA   See fah luto eetheen, ee yaba ma

    Dukey massa. Eeth wong che coh pa na

    Geen, nah meet' toe bunk' dunko. Lo choda!

HAN   O Jabba, thou wert e'er a kindly soul.

JABBA   Boska!

        [Exeunt Jabba and henchmen.

OBI-WAN   —Now if yon ship is truly fast,   60

    As quick as this Han Solo boasted so,

    We shall do well.

LUKE   *[spying ship:]*   —What folly-fallen ship

    Is this? What rough-hewn wayward scut is here?

HAN   Point-five past light speed shall she make, my lad.

    Now truly, earneth she low marks for looks,   65

    But still a finer spirit hath no ship.

    Full many small improvements have I made

    To render her e'en faster than before.

    Now, marry, gentlemen, if thou agree,

    We shall be off, and speedily, from here.   70

    [Aside:] And if thy mouth insulteth it again,

    I promise, boy, thy face shall meet my hand.

       [Chewbacca, Obi-Wan, Luke, C-3PO,

          and R2-D2 board ship.

CHORUS   But ere the ship departs the sandy dock,

    The stormtroopers appear with massive threat.

    Informèd by the beak'd spy's trait'rous talk,   75

    They come upon the ship, with weapons set.

Enter STORMTROOPERS.

TROOPER 5   Pray, stop yon ship! Aye, blast them to the stars!
HAN   Chewbacca, prithee, hence! Now let us go!
C-3PO   O, traveling in space, it works me woe!

                                              [Exeunt.

SCENE 4.

Space, aboard the Millennium Falcon.

CHORUS   Mos Eisley now is left behind at last,
             While newer scenes come into view apace.
             As Han's *Millenn'um Falcon* flies far fast
             The action of our play moves back to space!

Enter CHEWBACCA *and* HAN SOLO, *in ship*.

CHEWBAC.   Egh, auugh!
HAN   —Now are we follow'd hard upon   5
             By an Imperi'l cruiser. Verily,
             These passengers of great import must be
             For they by th'Empire hotly are pursu'd.
             Chewbacca, prithee, swift make our defense
             And angle the deflector shield whilst I   10
             Make plain the calculations for light speed.

Enter OBI-WAN KENOBI *and* LUKE SKYWALKER.

             Now vigilance, my Wookiee! Quickly come

Two further ships, to try and block our path.

LUKE   Nay, wherefore canst thou not outrun them both?

For thou didst boast of this strange vessel's speed.   15

HAN   [*aside:*] Again he prattles on about the ship!

O would that I had left him on the ground.

[*To Luke:*] Pray mark thy words, lad, else thou

surely wilt

Become like refuse to a Star Destroy'r

And float away to vanish midst the stars.   20

I'll warrant we shall soon in safety fly,

Once we the jump to hyperspace can make.

And what is more, my skill doth all exceed

At making keen maneuvers. All my life

Have I escap'd one scrape and yet one more.   25

Well I remember when—as but a boy—

I chas'd a nerf whilst on a speeder bike.

Through rocky field in harsh terrain we went,

Within, around and backward was our game.

I caught the nerf that splendid day, but aye,   30

It seems I have been dodging ever since.

OBI-WAN   How long, now, ere thou canst achieve lightspeed?

HAN   A few more moments shall it take whilst this

Computer doth its navigation work.

LUKE   But art thou mad? For certain they approach!   35

I have not made this journey just to die.

[*Aside:*] This man shall surely be the end of me.

HAN   The travel unto hyperspace is not

The same as thine a'dusting of the crops

Upon thy land of infinite dry sand.   40

Sans calculations quite exact, we would

Belike run through a belt of asteroids,
Or hit upon a planet's center mark.
Should such our fate become, thy trip would end
Before it had begun.

LUKE   —But O, what now?   45
What light through yonder flashing sensor breaks?

HAN   It marks the loss of yon deflector shield.
I bid thee, peace! Now sit and thou take heed,
For all's prepar'd to jump unto lightspeed.

CHORUS   Han graspeth quick the console in his hand,   50
Then suddenly the ship is bath'd in light.
With roar of engine—noise profound and grand—
The great *Millenn'um Falcon* takes her flight.

                       [Exeunt.

SCENE 5.

Inside the Death Star.

Enter GRAND MOFF TARKIN *and* ADMIRAL MOTTI.

MOTTI   Now are we come to th'system Alderaan.

Enter PRINCESS LEIA, *bound, with guards and* DARTH VADER.

LEIA   Ah! Gov'nor Tarkin, scurvy knave art thou.
Now seems it plain to me that Vader doth
Perform the part of docile dog unto
The sick'ning whinny of his Master's voice.   5
Familiar stench of dog's best friend have I

Mark'd deep within my sense of smell e'en when
I came unto this station.

TARKIN   —Ever wert
Thou charming, Leia, even to the last.
Thou couldst not comprehend how hard it was—   10
Aye, verily, how I did sigh and weep—
To give the order to destroy thy life.

LEIA   Surpris'd am I thou had the courage so
To take responsibility for such
As this unto thy cowardly, small self.   15

TARKIN   [aside:] She groweth ever bolder, which doth but
Increase my appetite to see her scream.
[To Leia:] My Princess, ere thou executed art,
I would thou join me for a moment full
Of pomp and circumstance. For at this grand   20
And noble ceremony shall the pow'r
Of this great battle station here be shown
To be quite fully operational.
Now no star system shall e'er dare oppose
The Emperor.

LEIA   —O but how wrong thou art!   25
The more that thou dost exercise thy grip,
The more star systems through that grip shall fall.

TARKIN   Not after we have shown the power vast
This battle station shall to them display.
And to the point: thou hast determin'd what   30
The prim'ry demonstration of its force
Shall be—which planet shall oblivion face.
[Aside:] Now shall I drive this nail unto its home,
And watch with joy as she with grief is torn.

	[*To Leia:*] Since thou hast so refus'd to grant to us	35
	The hid location of the rebel base,	
	I shall unleash this station's pow'r upon	
	Thine own home planet—even Alderaan.	
LEIA	Nay, do not so to peaceful Alderaan!	
TARKIN	Thou shalt a military target name,	40
	Then render swift the system's name as well.	
	Or else thy precious Alderaan goes to't.	
	I tire of asking o'er and o'er, so thus	
	I promise: this shall be the final time—	
	Where is thy rebel base?	
LEIA	—On Dantooine.	45
	They may be found on planet Dantooine.	
TARKIN	Ha, ha! Thou seest, Vader, how a cat	
	May have her claws remov'd. Now, Admiral,	
	Thou mayst continue with thy weapon's test,	
	And surely mayst thou fire when all's prepar'd.	50
LEIA	What madness here?!	
TARKIN	—Thou far too trusting art.	
	The tiny Dantooine is too remote	
	To show this station's pow'r but pray, fear not,	
	We shall in time thy rebel friends pursue.	
CHORUS	To do the Governor's most evil will,	55
	The people on the Death Star quickly rise.	
	With mighty flash, the beam bursts bright and shrill	
	And Alderaan is shatter'd 'fore their eyes.	
LEIA	[*sings:*] When Alderaan hath blossom'd bright,	
	Then sang we songs of nonny,	60
	But now her day is turn'd to night,	
	Sing hey and lack-a-day.	

My friend and I stood by the river,
Then sang we songs of nonny,
But I could not her soul deliver,   65
Sing hey and lack-a-day.
My planet hath the bluest shore,
Then sang we songs of nonny,
That noble land is now no more,
Sing hey and lack-a-day.   70

[*Exeunt.*

SCENE 6.

Space, aboard the Millennium Falcon.

Enter Obi-Wan Kenobi, Luke Skywalker, C-3PO, R2-D2,
and Chewbacca.

CHORUS   The instant Alderaan is smash'd to bits,
            Luke tries his lightsaber—a keen trainee.
            The droids and Wookiee play a game of wits,
            But Obi-Wan doth sense catastrophe.

OBI-WAN   [*aside:*] Now breaks my heart as through the
                                    Force I sense   5
            The suffering of many worthy souls.
            I know not what this doth portend, and yet
            I fear the worst.

LUKE   —Good Sir, how farest thou?

OBI-WAN   Forsooth, a great disturbance in the Force
            Have I just felt. 'Twas like a million mouths   10
            Cried out in fear at once, and then were gone,

All hush'd and quiet—silent to the last.
I fear a stroke of evil hath occurr'd.
But thou, good Luke, thy practice recommence.

         Enter HAN SOLO.

HAN   Thou mayest all thy troubles now forget,   15
            Th'Imperi'l knaves have been outrun at last.
            [*Aside:*] Well here's a solemn gathering indeed,
            Quite lacking in the proper gratitude.
            [*To Obi-Wan and Luke:*] Nay, speak thou not thy
                                   thanks too heartily,

Else shall thy praise go swiftly to my head.   20
But here's the point, we shall at Alderaan
Arrive ere long.

    [R2-D2 makes a move against Chewbacca
      in the game they play.

C-3PO   —Pray, R2, caution show.

R2-D2 Beep, whistle, squeak, beep, meep, hoo whistle.

CHEWBAC. —Auugh!

C-3PO A fair move hath he made, thou furry lump.
No use is there in screaming o'er the loss.   25
[*Aside:*] However did I join this company?
A Wookiee and his smuggler captain—O!

CHEWBAC. Egh.

HAN   —Be thou wise, droid, mark well what
        thou dost.
As it is said: black holes are worth thy fear,
But fear thou more a Wookiee's deadly wrath.   30

C-3PO But Sir, no proverb warns the galaxy
Of how a droid may hotly anger'd be.

HAN Aye, marry, 'tis because no droid hath e'er
Torn out of joint another being's arms
Upon a lesser insult e'en than this—   35
But Wookiees, golden droid, are not so tame.

C-3PO Thy meaning, Sir, doth prick my circuit board.
'Tis best to play the fool, and not the sage,
To say it brief: pray let the Wookiee win.

CHEWBAC. Auugh!

R2-D2 [*aside:*]   —Brute! The fool I'll play with
        thee, indeed.   40
Yet I perceive thou and thy friend have heart.

[Luke continues to practice with his lightsaber
against the remote.

OBI-WAN   Remember, Luke, the Force doth smoothly flow
            Within the feelings of a Jedi Knight.

LUKE   But doth the Force control one's ev'ry move?

OBI-WAN   'Tis somewhat so, but also shall the Force   45
            Obey thine every command, young Luke.

LUKE   [*aside:*] This Force, by troth, I'll never comprehend!
            It doth control and also doth obey?
            And 'tis within and yet it is beyond,
            'Tis both inside and yet outside one's self?   50
            What paradox! What fickle-natur'd pow'r!
            Aye: frailty, thy name—belike—is Force.
            [*To Obi-Wan:*] Alack! This small remote hath
                                   struck again!

HAN   Ha, ha! Thy errant systems of belief—
            Thy weapons ancient, all thy mysteries,   55
            Thy robes and meditations o'er the air,
            Thy superstitions, e'en thy precious Force—
            Cannot compare to my religion true:
            A trusty blaster ever by my side.
            With thus I say my prayers and guard my soul.   60

LUKE   Devoted foll'wer must thou be, with such
            A speech. Pray tell me, pilgrim reverent:
            Dost thou most truly disbelieve the Force?

HAN   A pilgrim, truly said! For I have gone
            From galaxy to galaxy and more,   65
            Yet never hath this faithful worshipper
            Found aught to recommend that strange belief—
            A single Force that binds the universe.

True 'tis, no power mystical controls
Han Solo's yet unfinish'd destiny.   70
And so I preach the one and only faith:
My simple, merry tricks are all my gods,
And nonsense is the only testament.
I worship at the shrine of my own will.

OBI-WAN   [*aside:*] A wise philosopher if e'er there was.   75
I'll warrant he hath character he hides.
[*To Luke:*] Now prithee, try again, and lay aside
Thy conscious self. Take thou this helmet thick,
Adorn thine eyes with silver shield opaque
And trust thine instincts only as thy guide.   80

LUKE   But surely 'tis a jest! For with this shield
I nothing now can see. How can I fight?
Aye, truly—fight or walk or even stand?
Without one's sight but little can be done.

OBI-WAN   Nay, 'tis in blindness one doth truly see!   85
For eyes deceive and sight is known to lie.
Let feelings be thy sight—their guidance trust!

CHORUS   With mind unsure Luke readies for the fight.
The small remote doth dodge most suddenly,
But with calm mind Luke blocks its lasers bright—   90
With inner eye the Force has let him see.

OBI-WAN   Hurrah! Thou canst do it!

HAN   —'Tis luck, no more.

OBI-WAN   Experience hath taught me much, dear man,
And none of it hath shown me aught of luck.

HAN   To find success against a small remote,   95
                       Is well, and taketh skill, I do confess.
                       To find success against a living soul,
                       However, also taketh excellence.

[Console beeps.

                       It seemeth we draw near to Alderaan.

[Exeunt Han Solo and Chewbacca.

LUKE   I did feel something, Obi-Wan, 'tis true.   100
                       It seems I fix'd my soul's eye on th'remote.

OBI-WAN   Seems, young one? Nay, thou didst! Think thou

                                             not seems.

                       Thou hast thy first step ta'en toward a world
                       Far greater than thou now canst understand.

[Exeunt Luke, C-3PO, and R2-D2.

                       And thus begins—if I have seen aright—   105
                       His transformation into Jedi Knight.

[Exit Obi-Wan.

SCENE 7.

Inside the Death Star.

Enter DARTH VADER *and* GRAND MOFF TARKIN.
Enter OFFICER CASS *opposite.*

CASS   My Lord, our scout ships have reach'd Dantooine.
              Remains of th'rebel base the scouts have found,
              Yet surely hath it been a length of time
              Deserted. Now shall they begin to search
              Surrounding systems, so to find the base.   5
                                        [Exit Officer Cass.

TARKIN   The wench hath lied! Deceiving, cut-throat girl,
              Most cunning princess born of Hell's own heart!

VADER   I knew full well she never would betray
              Her priz'd Rebellion whilst in her right mind.
              And thus I said: she ne'er should have our trust.   10

TARKIN   Destroy her! 'Tis a sentence more than just.
                                        [Exeunt.

SCENE 8.

Space, aboard the Millennium Falcon.

Enter HAN SOLO *and* CHEWBACCA.

HAN   Now dropping out of light speed's frantic rush
              We enter swift unto the area
              Where should there be great Alderaan in view.

But pray, what madness meets the *Falcon*'s flight?
Is this an ast'roid field I see before me?   5
The ship hath wrought a course direct and true,
And yet no Alderaan may here be found.
O errand vile, O portents of great ill!
What shall it mean, when planets are no more,
For those who make their wages by the stars?   10

Enter OBI-WAN KENOBI *and* LUKE SKYWALKER.

LUKE   What news, good Han?
HAN   —The ship's position hits
     The mark, and yet no Alderaan there is.
LUKE   I pray thee, marry, say: what canst thou mean?
     How can a planet vanish in the air?
HAN   Thou hast said right, my lad. It is not there.   15
     The planet's gone, all turned to rock and ash.
LUKE   Thou speak'st not right. Say how? Pray how?
                                     Tell how!
OBI-WAN   Destroy'd it was, and by the Empire cruel.
HAN   A thousand thousand ships could not destroy
     The planet. Truly 'twould take greater pow'r   20
     Than ever there was known to humankind.
     But soft! Another ship approaches quick.
     [A small ship flies quickly past the Millennium Falcon.
LUKE   Belike they can the tale to us relate.
OBI-WAN   Imperi'l fighter 'tis.
LUKE   —Hath it made chase?
OBI-WAN   Nay, nay! A short-range fighter 'tis. *[Aside:]* O how   25
     This situation here doth give me pause.

HAN   No base is there nearby. Whence cometh it?
            [*Aside:*] The courage in me melts away at this.
            My boasts cannot resolve this mystery.

LUKE   The ship departeth swiftly! If they have   30
            Identifi'd our lot, we shall have strife.

HAN   'Tis my intent to keep us from that Fate.
            Chewbacca, render its transmissions block'd.

OBI-WAN   Pray, let it go, 'tis too far flown.

HAN   —Not long!

OBI-WAN   Dost thou agree—a fighter of its size   35
            This deep in space could not have come alone?

LUKE   Belike 'twas in a group and now is lost.

HAN   It shall not live to tell the tale today.

LUKE   Forsooth! He makes his way to that small moon.

HAN   I may play checkmate on him ere he lands.   40

OBI-WAN   Alas—I sense the game, and we're the pawns.
            That is no moon. 'Tis a space station there.
            [*The Death Star looms in the distance, growing closer.*

HAN   'Tis far too large a space station to be.

LUKE   My feelings now do stir, I sense them well!
            They tell me we shall lose the match we play.   45

OBI-WAN   Pray, turn thee now the ship around.

HAN   —I shall!
            Now Chewie, lock thou quick th'auxill'ry pow'r.

LUKE   Why do we still approach? What can be done?

HAN   It hath th'advantage, using tractor beam
            To pull us in, unto its landing bay.   50

LUKE   But pray, some move thou must have left to make!

HAN   My moves are finish'd, lad, I must shut down,
            Else shall the ship entire soon come apart.

But still, with all my players I shall fight.

OBI-WAN　Thou canst not win, but will by strategy　　　55
Some good alternatives to fighting see.

CHORUS　So enters the *Millenn'um Falcon* in
Unto the Death Star, grand and stark and mean.
With fear the Wookiee and the three brave men
Look on as their space journey changes scene.　　　60
Meanwhile, the denizens within the base
Make haste to catch the ship that cometh near.
Commanders come with well-arm'd guards apace,
While stormtroopers do at their posts appear.

[Exeunt.

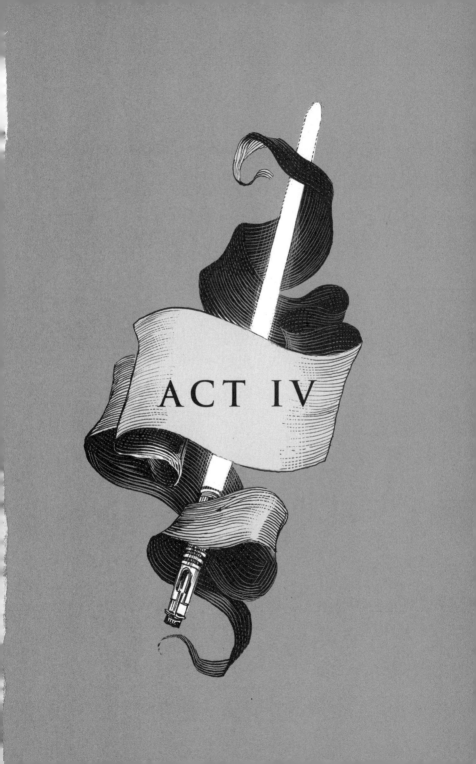

ACT IV

SCENE 1.

Inside the Death Star.

Enter DARTH VADER, GRAND MOFF TARKIN, *and* ENVOY.

ENVOY   A freighter hath been captur'd entering
            The system Alderaan. Its markings match
            A ship that hath Mos Eisley quickly fled.

VADER   This errant ship, belike, endeavors to
            Return the plans unto the princess who,   5
            Within this base, is lock'd in guarded cell.
            [*To Grand Moff Tarkin:*] Perhaps the princess yet
                                  hath use to us.

        [*Exit Grand Moff Tarkin. Vader crosses to the ship.*

Enter OFFICER 1, STORMTROOPERS, *and* GUARDS 1 *and* 2.

OFFICER 1   No person is aboard the ship, my Lord.
            The log maintain'd on board doth tell a tale
            Of all the crew abandoning the ship   10
            Directly after its departure. 'Tis
            No doubt a decoy, Sir. For all the pods
            Have launchèd been.

VADER   —Hast thou found any droids?

OFFICER 1   Nay, truly not, my Lord. If there had been,
            Then surely must they have abandon'd too.   15

VADER   Send thou a scanning crew aboard the ship,
            And check its nooks and crannies, ev'ry bit.

OFFICER 1   Aye, good, my Lord.

VADER   [*aside:*]   —Distract'd is my mind,
But through its cloudy haze the reason comes:
Unless I am in error, someone here   20
Has come. I have not felt this presence since
The days that are but dark in memory.
This presence I have known since I was young,
This presence that once call'd me closest friend,
This presence that hath all my hopes betray'd,   25
This presence that hath turn'd my day to night.
This awful presence present here must be,
So shall I to this presence violence
Present.

                                            [Exit Darth Vader.

OFFICER 1   —Now to thy work, and scan the ship!
TROOPER 5   The scan is done; no living soul is here.   30

                                    [Exeunt stormtroopers.

Enter OBI-WAN KENOBI, LUKE SKYWALKER, HAN SOLO,
CHEWBACCA, C-3PO, *and* R2-D2, *hidden.*

LUKE   'Tis fortunate thou hast these storage bins.
HAN   Their use hath ever been for smuggling goods.
Ne'er have I thought I would myself herein
Be smuggling. All we do is madness—fie!
If I could start the ship, the tractor beam   35
Would wrap its eagle's talons 'round my neck.
OBI-WAN   The tractor beam thou may'st leave unto me.
HAN   Thou fool, I knew that thou wouldst say as much.
OBI-WAN   Aye, say thou fool? Then fool, good Sir, am I.
But when thou sayest fool remember well   40

That fools do walk in foolish company.
So if I am a fool, perhaps 'tis true
That other fools around me may be found.
For who is he who hath more foolish been—
The fool or other fool who follows him?   45

  [*They hide. Guards 1 and 2 standby while scanning*
   crew enters ship and are bested by Obi-Wan, Luke,
     Han Solo, and Chewbacca.

GUARD 1 Oi! Didst thou hear that sound?

GUARD 2   —Pray, hear a sound?

GUARD 1 Aye, truly—I quite clearly heard a sound.

GUARD 2 Thine ears, mayhap, play tricks on thee, my friend.

GUARD 1 Nay, nay. Dost thou not think this strange?

GUARD 2   —What strange?

GUARD 1 The droids did flee the ship we have attack'd,   50
And unto Tatooine have gone by pod.
'Tis true, thus far?

GUARD 2   —I cannot claim 'tis false.

GUARD 1 On Tatooine they have been tracèd first
To Jawas vile and then to humans—

GUARD 2   —Dead.

GUARD 1 Aye, dead they are—our men did see to it.   55
But follow on: the boy who with them liv'd
Hath fled, we knew not where, till he was seen
At yon Mos Eisley with the pair of droids.

GUARD 2 Aye, aye, 'twas all in last week's briefing. Pray,
What more of this? Hast thou aught new to say?   60

GUARD 1 The boy and droids together disappear'd
The very hour the ship—this ship—did fly.
And now, the ship is here, though empty seems.

GUARD 2   Nay, empty 'tis! The scanning crew doth work
            E'en now.

GUARD 1   —Which bringeth me full circle to   65
            The sound I just have heard. Is't possible,
            My friend, that boy and droids and rebels all
            Have flown within this ship unto this base
            And yet—e'en now—whilst thou and I do speak,
            Still hide within the ship?

GUARD 2   —I am amaz'd!   70

GUARD 1   Aye, verily? Think'st thou I may be right?

GUARD 2   I said thou hast amaz'd me, and 'tis true.
            But never did I say I think thee right—
            Thou dost amaze by thy o'eractive thoughts!
            A hidden boy! The droids within! A fig!   75
            Avaunt, thou silly guard, be not so thick.
            Thy great imagination hath o'erwrought
            Thy better senses. Thinkest thou thy pow'rs
            Of judgment far exceed our Masters true?
            May'st thou outwit the great Darth Vader or   80
            The cunning of our Gov'nor Tarkin? Nay!
            We are but simple guards, our purpose here
            Is plain and to the point: we have been task'd
            To watch the ship and follow all commands,
            And not to prattle on with airy thoughts.   85

GUARD 1   Aye, thou hast spoke a well-consider'd word.
            Thou art a friend, as I have e'er maintain'd,
            And thou hast spoken truth and calm'd me quite.
            The rebels hide herein! What vain conceit!
            That e'er they should the Death Star enter—ha!   90

GUARD 2   It warms my heart to see thee so restor'd

And back to thine own merry, native self.

HAN   [*within:*] Pray, may we have thy good assistance here?

GUARD 1   [*to Guard 2:*] So, let us go together, friend. Good

cheer!

[*Guards 1 and 2 enter ship and are killed.*

Exeunt others.

SCENE 2.

Inside the Death Star.

Enter OFFICERS 2 *and* 3.

OFFICER 2   Say—TK-421, now wherefore hast

Thou left thy station? TK-421,

Canst thou my message hear? [*To Officer 3:*] Take

thou command,

Belike he hath a bad transmitter. So

Shall I attend and help him if I may.   5

Enter OBI-WAN KENOBI, C-3PO, R2-D2, *and* CHEWBACCA
with HAN SOLO *and* LUKE *dressed as stormtroopers, killing*
Officers 2 and 3.

CHORUS   Now through the doorway come our heroes brave.

Th'Imperi'l officers Chewbacca fights

Whilst Han with blaster doth his entry pave.

They have arriv'd: escape is in their sights.

CHEWBAC.   Auugh!

LUKE   —Fie! With all this howling nonsense and   10

With all thy blasting 'tis a miracle
That all within the station have not heard
Of our arrival.

HAN   —Surely, let them come!
A fight would I prefer to sneaking yon
And hither.

R2-D2   —Beep, beep whistle, squeak, beep,
                                           meep.   15

C-3PO   We have the outlet for the system found.
          [*Aside:*] O that my words might end their bickering.

OBI-WAN   'Tis well! Plug R2 in and he shall read
          The whole Imperi'l network.

R2-D2   —Beep, meep, squeak!
          Hoo, whistle, whee, ahh, beep, meep, squeak,
                                    beep, meep.   20

C-3PO   Now hath he found the main control unto
          The power beam that holds the ship herein.
          He shall attempt to show thee, presently,
          Where its exact location may be found.
          The tractor beam in seven places is   25
          Connected to the main reactor, but
          A power loss at any terminal
          Shall set the good *Millenn'um Falcon* free.

OBI-WAN   [*aside:*] That number seven shall our freedom mean.
          But only one of seven shall we need.   30
          I fear those numbers—seven and then one—
          Do something dangerous portend. But why?
          Our company is only six, unless
          There were another join'd unto us here.
          Then were we seven, yet what means the one?   35

O! Strangely sweeps the thought into my mind:
I have a feeling through the Force that ere
We leave this place, some seven shall we be.
Yet one shall stay behind as sacrifice.
Thus seven and thus one: the numbers tell   40
The story that herein shall soon be told.
[*To Luke and Han:*] Methinks ye two cannot assist

         me now.

This one—e'en I—shall go alone.
HAN   —Aye, good!
So shall I hearken unto what thou sayst,
For I already on this voyage have   45
Done more than that for which I have been paid.
LUKE I would go with thee, Sir.
OBI-WAN   —Pray, patience, Luke,
For thou must stay and guard the vital droids.
They must be taken safely to our friends,
Or other systems end like Alderaan.   50
Thy destiny, dear boy, doth truly go
Upon a path far different from mine,
And Fate for thee hath spun another thread
Than what she hath for Obi-Wan's life stitch'd.
The Force, it shall be with thee always, Luke.   55

       [*Exit Obi-Wan.*

LUKE [*aside:*] He hath bestow'd a Jedi's blessing here,
So why then am I utterly unnerv'd?
CHEWBAC. Auugh!
HAN   —Wookiee, thou hast spoken well
and true:
Whence hast thou this old bag of bones uncover'd?

LUKE   Yon Ben in all good virtues doth excel.   60
HAN   Aye, certain he excelleth when the goal
            Is but to lead us into trouble great.
LUKE   But thou hast not excell'd at offering
            A thought to how we can this station 'scape.
HAN   Yet any simple plan excelleth o'er   65
            Remaining here till all descend on us.
            It taketh not a wisdom that excels
            To know for certain fact that such is true.
R2-D2   [*aside:*] By heav'n I'll stop their bickering with this
            New information. [*To Han and Luke:*] Whistle,
                                beep, meep, whee!   70
LUKE   I prithee, what doth all this beeping mean?
C-3PO   Sir, I confess I do not know. He hath
            Declar'd that he hath found her, then the droid
            Repeats "She's here, she's here."
LUKE   —But, marry, who?
C-3PO   Good Princess Leia.
LUKE   —Princess Leia—here?   75
            [*Aside:*] Now doth this strange adventure stir my
                                blood!
HAN   What sayst of "princess"?
LUKE   —Where, thou droid? Say where!
HAN   What princess? On thy life, this thing unveil.
R2-D2   Beep, meep, meep, beep, squeak, whistle, beep,
                                meep, hoo.
C-3PO   E'en now the princess is on Level 5,   80
            Detention block of AA-23.
R2-D2   [*aside:*] O me! This new discovery of mine
            Doth shake my core, and shall arouse their souls.

               [*To Han and Luke:*] Meep, meep, ahh, beep, squeak,
                                  beep, meep, beep, ahh, nee.

C-3PO   I fear, good Sir, it doth give certain news   85
               The princess shall be terminated soon.

LUKE   Nay, nay! So quickly met and now, with this,
               So quickly lost! Now must we swiftly act!

HAN   What dost thou prattle on about? Pray tell!

LUKE   [*aside:*] O how can one describe in simple words   90
               The import this myster'ous woman hath
               Upon my life? [*To Han:*] The droids, these droids,
                                        are hers,
               She hath appear'd in message urgent, too!
               I see thou canst not understand it well,
               Yet what I know is this: we must give her   95
               Whate'er unflagging help and hope we may!

HAN   Speak not with such great folly. Obi-Wan
               Hath told us to remain.

LUKE   —Yet knew he not
               That she is here! [*To C-3PO:*] Pray tell me how
                                    we may
               Straight make our way to the detention block.   100

HAN   I say again what I have said before:
               To this location is my purpose fix'd
               And whether princess be within or no,
               I tell thee plain: I shall not thither go.

LUKE   She shall be executed! Thou hast said,   105
               Mere minutes past, that thou wouldst not remain
               To see our sudden, sure imprisonment.
               Now is thy fondest wish that we should stay?

HAN   To march to the detention block's unwise!

        To make our way to danger folly 'tis!   110
        To there present ourselves is passing mad!
        To boldly go where none hath gone is wild!

LUKE   Hast thou no heart? She sentenc'd is to die!

HAN   My sentence is: 'tis better she than I.

LUKE   [aside:] How shall I break a heart that loveth not,   115
        And how convince a man who lives by wits?
        He hath not seen the urgency within
        Her eyes. He hath not known the trembling in
        Her voice. He hath not heard the manner of
        Her plea. And yet, without his help I fear   120
        My errand surely fails. What shall I do?
        I know that under his exterior
        More good and noble aspirations lie.
        But by what tricks of speech to bring them forth,
        And what persuasions shall his fix'd will move?   125
        My aunt Beru hath told me once a tale:
        She said when first the deep, vast Kessel mines
        Were dug, it was revealèd that the pearls
        Of greatest value must by clever means
        Discover'd be. So did the miners band   130
        Together, so to make a useful tool.
        This tool would pull the pearls out of the rock
        In such a way they seem'd t'emerge by ruse.
        This practice had a name: the Hammer Ploy.
        Now shall I play a Hammer's Ploy upon   135
        The soul of this good smuggler, coaxing him
        By means most indirect to rescue good.
        Thus may the pearl of his still ragged soul
        Revealèd be and shine as ne'er before.

	[*To Han:*] I tell thee true: the lady wealthy is. 140
CHEWBAC.	Egh, auugh!
HAN	—Say, wealthy?
LUKE	—Wealthy, aye, with pow'r.
	If thou wouldst rescue her, thy great reward
	Would be—
HAN	—Pray, what?
LUKE	—Well more, I'll warrant, than
	Thou mayst imagine!
HAN	—Ha, thou josh with me.
	For my imagination hath few bounds. 145
LUKE	Thou shalt have it!
HAN	—So would I!
LUKE	—Aye, thou wilt!
HAN	Enough, I am engag'd. But I do hope
	Thou knowest well of what thou speakest here.
LUKE	Well, well!
HAN	—Hast thou a plan?
LUKE	—C-3PO,
	I prithee pass those binding cuffs to me. 150
	[*To Chewbacca:*] Good Wookiee, I shall put these on
	thee now.
CHEWBAC.	Auugh!
LUKE	—Han, perhaps thou shouldst that
	honor have.
	[*Han Solo cuffs Chewbacca.*
HAN	Fear not, dear Chewie, now his plan is plain.
C-3PO	My Master Luke, forgive my question frank:
	What should we do if we discover'd are? 155
LUKE	Lock thou the door.

HAN   —And pray they've blasters none.

C-3PO   [*aside to R-D2:*] 'Tis not a reassuring word.

R2-D2   —Beep, squeak!

                  [Exeunt C-3PO and R-D2 as Han, Luke,
                            and Chewbacca go to detention block.

CHORUS   So now Chewbacca, Han, and Luke proceed

             Unto detention level 5, quite grave.

             With bravery, good hope, and all Godspeed,   160

             Their errand is a princess there to save.

             The minions of the Death Star pay no mind,

             Nor are they by these three at all dismay'd.

             They do not fear the Wookiee, for behind

             Are Han and Luke as stormtroopers array'd.   165

             Meanwhile in stealth does Obi-Wan pass by

             And to the terminal doth make his way,

             But while he goes Darth Vader feels him fly—

             So ev'ry character his role doth play.

HAN   Thy plan, it shall not work.

LUKE   —And wherefore hast   170

             Thou not said this ere now?

HAN   —Aye, but I have!

          [Luke, Han Solo, and Chewbacca enter detention
                     block with Officer 4 and soldiers.

OFFICER 4   By heav'n, I say: where takest thou this thing?

LUKE   This pris'ner hath been transferr'd here, from cell

                           1-1-3-8.

OFFICER 4   —No one hath told me so.

             Thus 'tis my duty to confirm thy word.   175

                        [Soldiers approach.

CHEWBAC.   Auugh!

HAN —Be thou swift and merciless, good Luke!
[*Han Solo, Luke, and Chewbacca kill*
Officer 4 and soldiers.

CHORUS With blasters rais'd and targets in their scopes,
The three do overtake th'Imperi'l threat.
This obstacle o'ercome, they have fresh hopes—
But still their way hath not been made clear yet. 180

HAN Now shall we see wherein thy princess lies...
It saith herein she now is held in cell
2-1-8-7. Go! I'll hold them here.
[*To comlink:*] O be not anxious, comrades, fear ye not!
The situation here hath been controll'd. 185
All merry 'tis in the detention block!

OFFICER 1 [*through comlink:*] But what hath happen'd?

HAN —'Tis no matter, Sir—
A slight malfunction of the weapons here.
But all is well, and we are well, and all
Within are well. The pris'ners, too, are well, 190
'Tis well, 'tis well. And thou? Art also well?

OFFICER 1 [*through comlink:*] We shall dispatch a squad to verify.

HAN Nay, there's a leak in the reactor here.
Pray give us time to mend the matter well.
The leak is large and dangerous, but fear 195
Thou not, for all—I tell thee true—is well!

OFFICER 1 [*through comlink:*] But who art thou, and what's
thy number code?
[*Han Solo blasts comlink.*

HAN That conversation did my spirits bore!
Now Luke, prepare thyself for company!
[*Luke enters Princess Leia's chamber aside.*

LEIA	Thou truly art in jest. Art thou not small	200
	Of stature, if thou art a stormtrooper?	
	Does Empire shrink for want of taller troops?	
	The Empire's evil ways, I'll grant, are grand,	
	But must its soldiers want for fear of height?	
LUKE	[*aside:*] So hath my introduction fallen short.	205
	She sees the uniform, but not the man.	
	[*Removing helmet, to Leia:*] Luke Skywalker am I!	
	I have thy droids,	
	My noble errand is to rescue thee,	
	And I with Ben Kenobi have come here!	
LEIA	With Ben Kenobi? Where is he?	
LUKE	—Draw near!	210

[*Exeunt.*

SCENE 3.

Inside the Death Star.

Enter DARTH VADER *and* GRAND MOFF TARKIN.

VADER	I tell thee: he is here.	
TARKIN	—Old Obi-Wan	
	Kenobi? Wherefore dost thou think 'tis so?	
VADER	A tremor in the Force hath been my guide.	
	When last I felt its movement I was in	
	The presence of my former Master—he.	5
TARKIN	'Twas years ago. He must be dead by now.	
VADER	Thou shouldst not underestimate the pow'r	
	The Force doth hold.	

TARKIN	—The Jedi are extinct.
	Their power from the universe is gone
	And thou, dear friend, art all that doth remain 10
	Of their misguided, old religious ways.
	[*Comlink beeps.*] Pray, what?
OFFICER 1	[*through comlink:*] —Detention AA-23
	Hath sounded an emergency alert.
TARKIN	The princess? Fie! Put thou all sections on
	Alert.
VADER	—I tell thee: Obi-Wan is here, 15
	E'en now, and surely with him is the Force.
TARKIN	If thou art right, he must not be allow'd
	This station to escape. Nay, never, nay!
VADER	Escape is not his plan. I must confront
	My former Master, and must do't alone. 20

[Exit Grand Moff Tarkin.

The Master's lesson shall I teach in turn,
When Obi-Wan I face in battle soon.
I shall my vengeance win, my triumph gain,
When I deliver him unto his death.
Though comrades were we in full many wars,   25
Though friends we have been once, the past is gone—
And all is but a horrid memory.
Today my hopes shall be achiev'd when I
Strike down the vile betrayer of my youth.
This conflict shall fulfill my destiny,   30
And end for him in bleak eternity.

[Exit Darth Vader.

SCENE 4.

Inside the Death Star.

Enter HAN SOLO *and* CHEWBACCA, *with* STORMTROOPERS *entering*
and LUKE SKYWALKER *and* PRINCESS LEIA, *aside.*

CHORUS	With hearty blast th'Imperi'l troops appear—	
	Their coming doth require that Han retreat.	
	In moment dangerous, amidst great fear,	
	Here Han and Leia for the first time meet.	
HAN	Our exit's block'd now.	
LEIA	—With a fool's great skill	5
	Hast thou our route to freedom quite cut off.	
HAN	Mayhap Thy Highness would prefer her cell?	
LUKE	[*to comlink:*] C-3PO! Canst thou by any means	
	Discover how we may the cellblock leave?	
	Our entry point is now a deadly end.	10
C-3PO	[*through comlink:*] All to thy presence have	
	alerted been!	
	The entrance only takes one in or out.	
	All other information where thou art	
	Hath been restricted.	
LUKE	[*to Han:*] —Now are we quite trapp'd!	
HAN	I cannot hold them back forever, sure!	15
LEIA	'Tis quite a rescue thou hast plann'd for me.	
	Thou hast come in, but how shalt thou go out?	
	Hath folly been thy guide?	
HAN	—He hath the plan,	
	Not I, thou sweetheart of ingratitude!	

[*Leia takes Luke's blaster, shoots hole in wall.*

By what dark sprite of Hell art thou possess'd?   20

LEIA   It falls to me to make our rescue good.

Now follow me into the refuse heap!

[*Princess Leia exits into chute.*

HAN   [*to Chewbacca:*] Go thou hence!

CHEWBAC.   —Auugh!

HAN   —Get in, thou furry lump!

I care not what thou smell'st within! Unless

'Tis death, must be a sweeter smell than this   25

Attack! Now go, be not afear'd, my friend!

[*Chewbacca exits into chute.*

[*To Luke:*] I say, what charming girl thou here

                                        hast found!

I either shall destroy her, or, perhaps,

I may in time begin to like the wench!

LUKE   [*aside:*] Nay, executioner or lover, both   30

Are far too great a role for thee to play.

HAN   Now go, and follow I, all else be damn'd!

[*Exeunt Luke and Han into chute.*

CHORUS   The scene doth shift unto the refuse space,

Where all is rot, as like a fun'ral pyre.

Though safe, our heroes other woes now face—   35

They go from frying pan unto the fire.

Enter HAN SOLO, CHEWBACCA, LUKE SKYWALKER, *and*
PRINCESS LEIA *in garbage pile at bottom of chute.*

CHEWBAC.   Auugh!

HAN   —O! What wonder of the human mind

Hath thought to bring us here? Your Highness must
Be lauded greatly for discov'ring such
A wondrous smell as this! [*To Chewbacca:*] I'll blast
          the door, 40
Swift get thee hence!

LUKE   —Nay, prithee, shoot thou not!
      [Han shoots and the blast ricochets.
Thou arrant knave! Wouldst thou undo us all?
I have already tried to exit thus,
But lo, as thou now plainly seest, thou brute,
The passageway is seal'd magnetic'lly! 45

LEIA Now rid us of that blaster, quickly too—
Else shall thine edgy trigger finger mean
The certain death of all of us herein!

HAN O, aye, thy Worship—ha! 'Twas all in my
Control till thou didst lead us to this heap, 50
Nor shall the stormtroopers need any time
To calculate where all of us have flown.

LEIA And yet, I say to you: it could be worse.
        [A loud sound is heard.

HAN 'Tis worse.

LUKE   —I'll warrant, something lives in here!

HAN [*aside:*] I 'spect his word is true, but fear to say. 55
[*To Luke:*] 'Tis but thy keen imagination, Luke.

LUKE 'Twas not just my imagination that
Hath now swum boldly past my leg, or else
Imagination now hath body too!
Aye there—did thine eyes see? Did but a mere 60
Imagin'd figment just swim by?

HAN   —See what?

> *[Luke is pulled into the water by an unseen force.*

CHORUS   Yet ere young Luke with answer can respond,
              He's pull'd unto the wat'ry depths below.
              For sev'ral moments in that garbage pond
              No sign is seen beneath the murky flow.   65
              An om'nous sound breaks forth into the pit,
              And seconds later Luke emerges, spent.
              The beast's pursuit of him for now is quit—
              A greater challenge doth this represent.

> *[Luke rises above the surface.*

LEIA   O miracle, that thou art truly sav'd!   70
              What happen'd there, below the briny sludge?

LUKE   I do not know. The slimy creature hath
              Releas'd its vice-like grip on me and fled.

> *[Another sound is heard.*

HAN   I have a feeling bad about this sound.

> *[The walls begin to contract.*

LUKE   The walls—O horrid Fate—begin to move!   75

LEIA   Be not afear'd, and stand thou not in awe,
              But rouse thee now and halt its sure approach!
              Now lend me thy assistance!

CHEWBAC.   —Auugh!

LUKE   —But wait,
              I have a comlink and may hail the droids.
              [*Into comlink:*] C-3PO! Say, art thou there? Pray,
                                                    speak!   80

CHORUS   But while he tries to hail the golden droid,
              C-3PO hath troubles of his own,
              For stormtroopers are to their room deploy'd
              And now the droids must save themselves alone.

Enter C-3PO *and* R2-D2 *aside, with* STORMTROOPERS.

C-3PO   O grant us help, for there are madmen here,   85
              Who have e'en now to th'prison level gone!
              If thou but hurry, thou may'st catch them there.

R2-D2   [*aside:*] Well said, my friend! He hath a merry wit
              When pride and scorn fall not from out his mouth.

TROOPER 7   [*to other stormtroopers:*] Aye, prithee fellows,
                          come and follow me!   90
                      [*Exeunt stormtroopers.*

CHEWBAC.   Egh.

LUKE   —3PO!

HAN   —Now climb on top!

LEIA   —In faith,
              I try!

LUKE   —Where is the knave? C-3PO!

C-3PO   I fear a wicked fate's befallen them.
              Pray, R2, see if they imprison'd are.
              Now search apace!

R2-D2   —Beep, squeak, meep, whistle, beep!   95

HAN   One thing is certain: we shall thinner be.
              I shall not lose my wit, e'en in death's face!

R2-D2   Beep, beep.

C-3PO   —They are not found, O great relief!
              Where may they be?

R2-D2   —Squeak.

C-3PO   —Use the comlink? O!
              I had forgotten quite, and turn'd it off.   100
              [*Into comlink:*] Pray, art thou there, Sir?

LUKE   [*into comlink:*]   —3PO? 'Tis thou?

C-3PO   [*into comlink:*] I will confess: we have some
                                        problems fac'd.

LUKE   [*aside, into comlink:*] Peace, 3PO! Lend ears and
                                        not thy voice!

              Disarm thou ev'ry refuse masher on
              Detention levels! Dost thou mark me, droid?   105
              Be rapid, else thy Master is no more!

C-3PO   [*aside, to R2-D2:*] Nay, shut them all down!
                                        Hurry, R2, go!

R2-D2   Beep, squeak, meep, whistle, hoo.

LUKE   —Ahh!

HAN   —O!

LEIA   —Ahh!

CHEWBAC.   —Auugh!

C-3PO   No heart within this golden breast doth beat,
              For only wires and circuit boards are here.   110
              Yet as I hear my Master's dying screams
              No heart is necessary for my grief.
              A droid hath sadnesses, and hopes, and fears,
              And each of these emotions have I felt
              Since Master Luke appear'd and made me his.   115
              No Master have I e'er respected so,
              Thus at this moment grave I do declare:
              There is no etiquette for shedding tears,
              No protocol can e'er express my woe.

R2-D2   [*aside:*] A plague on 3PO for action slow,   120
              A plague upon my quest that led us here,
              A plague on both our circuit boards, I say!

LUKE   [*into comlink:*] Nay, nay, fear not, dear droid,
                                        we all still live!

Pray open thou the door on maint'nance hatch
3-2-6-8-2-7—blessèd be!   125

R2-D2   [*aside:*] O fondest hope, O fervent pray'rs now heard!
My Master is alive, and plagues deterr'd!

[*Exeunt all.*

SCENE 5.
Inside the Death Star.

Enter OBI-WAN KENOBI *in stealth, with two* STORMTROOPERS
and power terminal.

CHORUS   While Luke and Leia, Han and Chewie flee,
Old Obi-Wan has reached the power source.
He cuts the tractor beam quite cunningly,
Then makes his exit drawing on the Force.

TROOPER 8   What do these warnings tell—shall we explore?   5

TROOPER 9   Belike 'tis just a drill, and nothing more!

[*Exeunt.*

SCENE 6.

Inside the Death Star.

Enter Luke Skywalker, *holding stormtrooper helmet.*

LUKE   Alas, poor stormtrooper, I knew ye not,
            Yet have I ta'en both uniform and life
            From thee. What manner of a man wert thou?
            A man of inf'nite jest or cruelty?

A man with helpmate and with children too?   5
A man who hath his Empire serv'd with pride?
A man, perhaps, who wish'd for perfect peace?
Whate'er thou wert, good man, thy pardon grant
Unto the one who took thy place: e'en me.

Enter HAN SOLO, CHEWBACCA, *and* PRINCESS LEIA.

HAN   If we may female-giv'n advice avoid,   10
             We should be well upon our merry way.
LUKE   Aye, stand I ready to be gone from here.
                                 [*Large sound is heard.*
CHEWBAC.   Auugh!
HAN   —Say, where dost thou go to, Wookiee?
                                                      Where?
                                              [*Han fires.*
LEIA   Thou brute, they shall o'erhear!
HAN   —Pray come thou here,
             Chewbacca, else I brand thee cowardly.   15
LEIA   Now use thine ears and, if thou hast, thy brain:
             I know not who thou art or whence thou cam'st,
             Yet from this moment, thou shalt heed my words.
HAN   Your Worship, prithee let me be direct:
             I have one Lord and Master: 'tis myself,   20
             And only from that one take I commands.
LEIA   A wonder great that thou art still alive!
             Now prithee, shall this walking carpet be
             Removèd from my path?
HAN   [*aside:*]   —A saucy wit!
             A wicked tongue that will be tam'd, I vow—   25

No other payment is reward enough.
                        [They come upon the hangar where the
                             Millennium Falcon *is held.*
[To Luke, Princess Leia, and Chewbacca:] There 'tis.

LUKE	*[into comlink:]* —C-3PO? Say, art thou there?
C-3PO	*[aside, in comlink:]* Aye, Sir.
LUKE	*[into comlink:]* —And art thou safe?
C-3PO	*[aside, in comlink:]* —For now, we are.

We are position'd in the hangar just
Across, directly, from the gallant ship.   30

LUKE   *[into comlink:]* And we are just above thee, so stand by.

LEIA   *[to Han:]* Hast thou come here in that ungainly heap?
Thou art, perhaps, then braver than I thought.

HAN   'Tis well and good, though I need not thy praise.
Now let us hence, and to the ship repair!   35

CHORUS   The foursome t'ward the ship with swift foot race,
But soon they meet with opposition dire.
Chewbacca goes with Han, both giving chase,
While Luke and Leia to other paths aspire.

HAN   *[running away:]* Fly hence, my friends, and meet
                            us at the ship!   40
                     [Exeunt Han Solo and Chewbacca,
                          chasing stormtroopers.

LEIA   A lion's share of courage hath he not?

LUKE   *[aside:]* Alas! Now is her heart mov'd unto him?
[To Leia:] What help is courage if it leads to death?
But come now, let us flee another way.

CHORUS   The chase is under way as all make haste!   45
Han—once pursuer—soon becomes pursu'd

When with a mass of stormtroopers he's fac'd:
He turneth quick as like a man unglu'd.
Meanwhile the princess and young Luke do flee
From troopers coming after them with speed.   50
They happen on an open door and see
A chasm past which they cannot proceed.

LUKE   Belike we have an errant corner turn'd,
For this deep hole leads not unto the ship!

LEIA   Forsooth, methinks that we shall safer be—   55
E'en with the pit—behind a door shut fast.

[She shuts door.

Yet now I see no lock we may employ,
So what for our dear freedom is the key?

[Luke Skywalker shoots door control.

LUKE   [*aside:*] I take a note from Han and blaster use,
Belike that shall keep enemies at bay.   60

LEIA   We must o'erleap this deep abyss somehow.
Pray, canst thou use thy sharp and earnest wit
To find a means for lengthening the bridge?

LUKE   O! Now the wisdom of old Obi-Wan
Is proven, for the blaster was too harsh.   65

LEIA   Do something, prithee, or they shall burst through!

CHORUS   So clever Luke the scene he doth survey
And soon conceives a noble plan to cross.
To take their flight and save them sans delay,
He bares a length of rope as thin as floss.   70
Attack'd, now Leia matches fire with fire,
And so they cross, a'swinging o'er th'abyss.
But ere they fly, the princess doth inspire
More strength in Luke by means of royal kiss.

LEIA   A kiss for luck before our flight, dear friend,   75
              A kiss upon thy cheek from lips of mine,
              A kiss to give thee hope and confidence,
              A kiss to bring us courage in this time.
              Now take this kiss—my gift bestow'd by choice—
              And on the other side we'll soon rejoice.   80

                                                    [*Exeunt.*

SCENE 7.

Inside the Death Star.

CHORUS   While droids do worry o'er their Master's fate,
              Han and Chewbacca make their swift escape.
              While Luke and Leia now in safety wait,
              A mighty, final duel taketh shape.

              Enter DARTH VADER *and* OBI-WAN KENOBI,
                  with STORMTROOPERS *watching.*

VADER   For certain, I have waited, Obi-Wan,   5
              And now at last we meet together here:
              Our destinies once and for all fulfill'd.
              The circle of our lives is now complete—
              A student was I when I left thee last,
              But now I am the Master over thee.   10
OBI-WAN   Thou art a Master, Darth, I know 'tis true,
              But only evil hast thou Master'd yet.
                                              [*They duel.*
VADER   In time thy pow'rs have weak become, old man.

OBI-WAN	And yet thou canst not win, I'll warrant, Darth.
	For if thou strike me down, e'en now, e'en here, 15
	I shall more great and powerful become
	Than e'er thou hast imagin'd possible.
VADER	I tell thee plain: thou shouldst not have return'd.
CHORUS	What noble battle passes twixt these men—
	Lightsabers rage from Sith and Jedi Knight! 20
	No more courageous battle hath there been:
	'Tis like the day does combat with the night.
	Now whilst the two in conflict strike their blows,
	The others come that they the ship may find.
	At first Han Solo with Chewbacca shows, 25
	Then Luke and Princess Leia just behind.

Enter HAN SOLO, *with* CHEWBACCA *aside.*

HAN	Did we not just this fright'ning party leave?

Enter LUKE SKYWALKER *and* PRINCESS LEIA *with them.*

	Where hast thou been?
LEIA	—We did some old friends meet,
	But, finding them unfriendly, have both vow'd
	To find far truer, better friends henceforth. 30
LUKE	Hast thou seen any problems with the ship?
HAN	It seemeth fine, if we may make approach
	And get beyond the stormtroopers. Aye, then
	My fondest hope is that thine Obi-Wan
	Hath vanquishèd the wicked tractor beam. 35
LUKE	Behold, what ease! The stormtroopers go hence.

C-3PO	Now 'tis our chance, good R2-D2, come.
R2-D2	[*aside:*] Aye, will he now be leading me?
	[*To C-3PO:*] Beep, squeak!
HAN	Fly, fly, good friends! Unto the ship make haste.
CHORUS	As ev'ryone unto the ship draws nigh, 40
	Young Luke sees Obi-Wan trade slice with slice.
	And Ben Kenobi, catching young Luke's eye,
	Prepares to make a gracious sacrifice.
OBI-WAN	A Jedi is not made of fear or hate,
	But must a nobler countenance display. 45
	It is a lesson learn'd in times gone by
	That still I teach myself unto this day.
	Full many years I've spent with thoughts of this—
	This instant when Darth Vader I'd confront.
	But now my thirst for retribution's cold, 50
	While sweet forgiveness doth my spirit taste.
	I know I cannot win this battle here,
	Nor would I wish to slay the kindly man
	Who surely still within this black shell lives.
	And so, unto this death I'll go, this sleep, 55
	This sleep that promises the dream of peace.
	This undiscover'd galaxy wherein
	I'll know at last tranquility of heart.
	But ere I die, I'll one last lesson teach.
	I shall in this—my final moment—set 60
	A keen example for the universe,
	That future generations may yet know
	The valor and the strength of Jedi Knights.
	Put up thy lightsaber now, Obi-Wan,
	And show thyself a Jedi to this son. 65

                                    [Obi-Wan raises lightsaber and is killed
                                                by Darth Vader.

CHORUS   The cry of "Nay!" escapes Luke's trembling lip
                And stormtroopers turn 'round to see them there.
                A battle great begins before the ship
                As to the *Falcon* these brave souls repair.
                But ere the group departs amid the fray,   70
                Luke hears the voice of Obi-Wan inside:
                "Pray run, Luke run," the inner voice doth say,
                And Luke the Death Star leaves with Force as guide.
                                                [Exeunt.

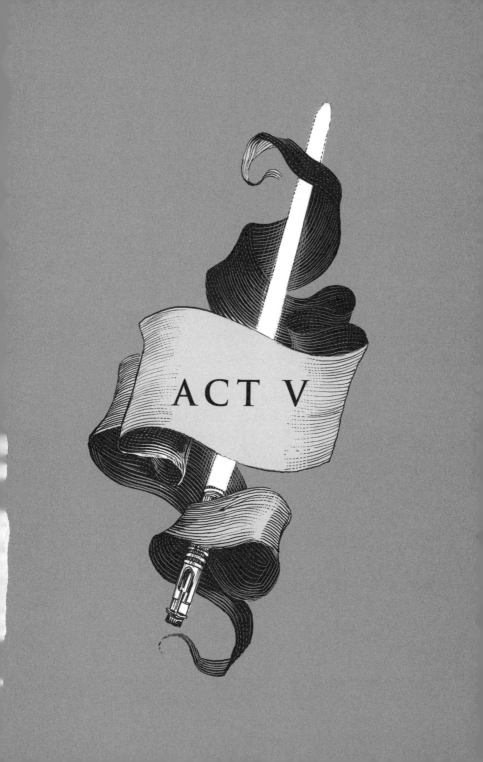

ACT V

SCENE 1.

Space, aboard the Millennium Falcon.

Enter LUKE SKYWALKER *and* PRINCESS LEIA *separately,*
with C-3PO *and* R2-D2.

LUKE   My heart doth break at this most recent loss,
            And how shall heart be heal'd of this grave pain?
            My aunt and uncle first, and now this Ben:
            Did e'er a person know such grief as mine?

LEIA   His heart breaks for a person, Obi-Wan—   5
            My heart breaks for a people, Alderaan.
            My ship crush'd first, and now my planet too:
            Did e'er a person know such grief as ours?

LUKE   I have but known this man a little time,
            Yet in my heart he holds a special place.   10
            So had I hop'd to learn from him the Force,
            And be his eager new apprentice too.

LEIA   My Alderaan I've known for all my life,
            And hold it in my heart in high'st esteem.
            So had I hop'd to one day make it home,   15
            When this rebellion all is pass'd away.

LUKE   But now must I another pathway take
            And make my final destiny sans him.
            My hopes shall not fulfillèd be as plann'd,
            Yet may I hope to serve through diff'rent deeds. 20

LEIA   But now must I some other course adopt
            And write my life's own story without them.
            My dreams shall not be realiz'd as I wish'd,

    Yet may I dream to see some other Fate.

LUKE   Thus shall I strive to hold my head up high,   25
    And be a beacon to this princess dear.
    So I'll in her Rebellion play my part
    And show her what a Jedi Knight may be.

LEIA   Thus shall I strive to hold my hands outstretch'd
    And be a calming presence to this man.   30
    So I'll in his deep mourning act my role
    And show him what a comfort friends may be.

HAN   [*within:*] We now approach the Empire's sentry ships,
    I prithee, Chewie, keep the ships at bay
    And angle our deflector shields whilst I   35
    Do charge the weapons for our sure defense!

      [He enters and speaks to Luke and Leia.

    My friends, I know ye grieve most heartily,
    Yet we have not made our escape complete.
    I need thy help, so get thee to the guns!

CHORUS   With newfound strength Luke rises to the chore 40
    And finds the console opposite from Han.
    With lasers arm'd and engines all a'roar,
    TIE fighters swiftly come—the battle's on!

HAN   Now be thou sharp, young Luke.

LEIA   —They come anon!

LUKE   They come too fast, how shall we hold them off? 45

LEIA   The ship is struck! All lateral controls
    Have been destoy'd.

C-3PO   —O heav'n! *[He falls.*

HAN   —Be not afear'd.
    I'll warrant that the ship shall surely hold.
    [*Aside:*] O ship, hast heard my word? I prithee, hold!

LUKE	Now have I smash'd one!
HAN	—Well, thou worthy lad! 50
	[*Aside:*] But be thou not too full of pride and joy.
	When battle's won then mayst thou boast indeed,
	But none e'er boasted yet who bested were!
LEIA	Still two remain, so be thou bold and wise.
CHORUS	With shouts and sweat and ev'ry skill employ'd, 55
	Young Luke and Han contend with all their might.
	At length, the last TIE fighter is destroy'd
	And battle ends in fiery blast of light.
LUKE	We are the victors—merry is the day!
C-3PO	But I have fallen—help, O help me now. 60
	'Tis surely thy fault, R2-D2, see!
R2-D2	Beep, meep, squeak, whistle, beep, meep, whistle,

                                      whee.

                                  [Exeunt.

SCENE 2.

Inside the Death Star.

Enter GRAND MOFF TARKIN *and* DARTH VADER.

TARKIN	Now have they gone? The rebels truly fled?
VADER	They have—e'en now—the jump to light speed made.
TARKIN	And thou art sure—I prithee, say thou art—
	The homing beacon safe aboard the ship
	Hath placèd been? I fear this risk's unwise. 5
VADER	The risk and homing beacon both have been
	Well plac'd. Thou, Tarkin, be assur'd thereon.

TARKIN   'Tis well, good friend, I trust thy word herein,
                Yet would I have thee know what danger's here:
                While I have risk'd the world to let them flee,   10
                Since thou dost reassure, the risk's on thee.

                                                      [Exeunt.

SCENE 3.

Space, aboard the Millennium Falcon.

Enter HAN SOLO *and* PRINCESS LEIA.

HAN   Thy rescue hath been wondrous, think'st thou not?
             Say I: at times I do myself amaze.
             Amazing hath my rescue of thee been,
             Amazing is my hand at piloting,
             Amazing all my part in this escape,   5
             Amazing—aye, 'tis true—my handsome looks.
LEIA   Amazing is thy pride and love of self!
             Thus stand I now amaz'd that e'er thou shouldst
             Allow thy great, amazing self to stoop
             So low that thou wouldst rescue such as I.   10
             But let me now amaze thee if I may,
             By telling thee that thy amazement is
             Misplac'd! For never have Imperi'l ships
             Let enemies escape with such great ease
             As thou and thy amazing vessel have   15
             Just now amazingly escap'd.
HAN   —Nay, nay!
             Call'st thou this venture easy, Princess? Pish!

LEIA	I'll warrant we are being track'd e'en now.
HAN	This ship shall never trackèd be, good sis.
LEIA	Methinks thou dost upon this vessel far 20
	Too great a trust bestow. But none of that,
	I merely am reliev'd that R2 doth
	The information safely in him guard.
HAN	But wherefore does this matter, Princess, say:
	What carries he?
LEIA	—Rebellion's greatest hope: 25
	For he doth hold the readouts technical
	Unto that battle station, aye, the one
	That such great pow'r display'd o'er Alderaan.
	My hope it is that when the data can
	Be read, an inner weakness we shall find. 30
	Though thou hast seen this battle end, the war
	Has not concluded yet.
HAN	—But there thou err'st,
	Thou dost not speak my mind. For this ship and
	Its pilot, Princess, 'tis concluded now.
	I have not join'd thy revolution, nay— 35
	My purpose runs not to Rebellion help,
	My purpose runs not to assist thyself.
	My purpose runs toward one aim alone,
	And I do speak it plain: I shall be paid,
	And will be paid, and ev'ry aspect of 40
	My being lives in expectation of
	The moment when thou shalt my coffers fill.
LEIA	O fiendish knave! Be thou concernèd not
	O'er thy reward. If thou in money dost
	Find love, then surely shalt thou have it, aye. 45

Enter LUKE SKYWALKER.

Thy friend is ev'ry part a hirèd man,
A mercenary with no mercy, he.
I question whether he doth care for aught   50
Or anyone.

                                        [*Exit Princess Leia.*

LUKE   [*aside:*]   —But I do care, I do!
If only, Leia, thou didst know how much.
[*To Han:*] Pray tell me, Han, what dost thou think
                                                  of her?

HAN   I tell thee true, my mind is settl'd fast
When it thinks not of her.

LUKE   —'Tis well, 'tis well.   55

HAN   [*aside:*] Now is it plain to me why he doth ask!
The boy doth fancy her, I'll warrant, else
I've made a great mistake in judgment here.
What use are young men's dreams if not for mocking?
So I shall dance upon his tender heart: 60
[*To Luke:*] And yet—

LUKE   [*aside:*]   —Alas, a "yet"? What's this of
                                                  "yet"?

HAN   The woman truly hath a spirit bold,
And yet I know not. What think'st thou, I pray:
Think'st thou a princess could with me be—

LUKE   —Nay.

                                        [*Exeunt.*

SCENE 4.
The rebel base on Yavin IV.

CHORUS   The swift *Millenn'um Falcon* makes its course
                     Unto the place the Empire long has sought:
                     On Yavin IV rebellion hath its source,
                     O'er which the final battle shall be fought.

Enter PRINCESS LEIA *and* COMMANDER WILLARD, *with*
LUKE SKYWALKER, HAN SOLO, *and* R2-D2 *behind.*

WILLARD   Good Princess, thou art safe! When word we heard   5
                     About the cruel destruction of thy home
                     We fear'd the worst. But now to see thee safe
                     Is like a fragrant blossom to my sense.
LEIA   In time we may recount our griefs, good Sir,
                     But now is the occasion we must act.   10
                     I prithee, take this R2 unit here
                     And use the data thou shalt find therein
                     To plan our great attack. Our only hope
                     It is, Commander, trust in what I say.
CHORUS   The records R2 holds are analyz'd,   15
                     And lo, an opportunity appears!
                     The rebels straight are of the news appris'd
                     And hearts made ready as the battle nears.
                     But whilst they mine good R2's database,
                     The Empire learns where all the rebels wait.   20
                     The Death Star makes its way unto the place
                     To bring to Yavin Alderaan's grim fate.

Enter GENERAL DODONNA, WEDGE ANTILLES, *and various rebel*
commanders and pilots.

DODONNA   Now gather 'round, ye pilots good and true,
               For here shalt thou a goodly lesson learn.
               We have a single hope in this attack,   25
               And ye shall hear how we may compass it:
               The battle station heav'ly shielded is,
               And hath more pow'r to fire than half our fleet.
               It hath defenses 'gainst a large assault,
               But like the king who fell for want of horse   30
               This station may be crush'd by smaller might.
               A one-mann'd fighter may have strength to clear
               The outer walls and penetrate therein.
GOLD LEAD.   Beg pardon, Sir, but how—I prithee—shall
               A one-mann'd fighter stand its ground 'gainst that?   35
DODONNA   A question ask'd in wisdom 'tis, good friend.
               The Empire vast hath not consider'd small
               Snub fighters to be any threat, methinks,
               Else surely 'twould make suitable defense.
               The strongest people often put their faith   40
               Upon their strength alone, yet often such
               As these are bested by a people led
               By wisdom, skill and cunning. To the point:
               The plans provided by the princess show
               The battle station's fatal weakness, aye.   45
               A weakness do I call it, yet be sure:
               The hard approach therein shall per'lous be.
               Thou must maneuver through the trench above
               The surface unto this especial point:

There shalt thou find the glory spot, my lads,   50
There shalt thou with a blast most keenly shot
Bring down an Empire cruel and merciless.
But take ye heed, for all is not yet told:
The hole thou must attempt to strike is but
Two meters wide, a thermal pipe for waste.   55
This hole shall make thy laser's power grow,
This hole shall start a chain reaction great,
This hole, if thou canst hit it, wins the day—
This hole shall end the battle station whole.

GOLD LEAD.   But Sir, the odds of such a hit are nil.   60

WEDGE   'Tis near impossible. Shall we, I say,
Attempt this madness or, mayhap 'tis best
If we do live to fight another day.
If we had but another thousand ships—

LUKE   Friends, rebels, starfighters, lend me your ears.   65
Wish not we had a single fighter more,
If we are mark'd to die, we are enough
To make our planets proud. But should we win,
We fewer rebels share the greater fame.
We all have sacrific'd unto this cause.   70
Ye all know well the fam'ly I have lost—
My uncle dear and aunt belov'd, aye both,
And then a mentor great, a pow'rful friend.
As massive is the grief I feel for them,
I know full well they'd not have me back down.   75
The princess hath a planet lost, with friends
And family alike—how great her pain!
And yet as grave as that emotion is,
She knoweth they would have her lead us still.

And ye, ye goodly men and women too,   80
Ye all have liv'd and lov'd and lost as well,
Your stories are with mine one and the same.
For all of us have known of grief and joy,
And every one has come unto this day
Not so that we may turn our backs and flee,   85
But that we may a greater courage show,
Both for ourselves and those we left behind.
So let us not wish further ships were here,
And let us not of tiny holes be fear'd—
Why, I have with a T-16 back home   90
Gone hunting womp rats scarcely larger than
The target we are call'd upon to strike.
And ye, ye brave souls, have your memories
Of your great exploits in your own homelands,
So think on them and let your valor rise,   95
For with the Force and bravery we win.
O! Great shall be the triumph of that hour
When Empire haughty, vast and powerful
Is fell'd by simple hands of rebels base,
Is shown the might of our good company!   100
And citizens in Bespin now abed,
Shall think themselves accurs'd they were not here.
For never shall rebellion see a time
More glori'us than our strong attack today!

ALL   Aye!
DODONNA   —Go ye then, and Force be with you all!   105

     [Exeunt all but Luke Skywalker.

CHORUS   A bustling preparation now is made,
As ev'ry man unto his post does go.

A joyful spirit doth the base pervade,
Whilst on the Death Star pride doth overflow.

Enter DARTH VADER *with* GRAND MOFF TARKIN, *aside in Death Star.*

VADER   This day, I'll warrant, lives in history: 110
               The end of old Kenobi it hath seen,
               And end of the Rebellion draweth near.
                         [*Exeunt Darth Vader and Grand Moff Tarkin.*

                         Enter HAN SOLO.

LUKE   Now what is this? Thou hast thine only love—
               Thy dear reward—and now thou leavest quick?
HAN   'Tis true, I do confess. For I shall ne'er   115
               Be free unless I use this great reward
               To clear me from the crushing weight of debt.
               And be thou honest, should I here remain
               To fight against a pow'r as great as this?
               'Tis foolishness, this fight, 'tis lunacy.   120
               Pray Luke, come thou with us! Thou art a brave
               And worthy lad, with wit and strength to fight.
LUKE   Speak thou not so! But open up thine eyes!
               See here what noble cause thou leav'st behind!
               Look in the hearts of these good people here!   125
               Behold the Force that keeps rebellion strong!
               Thou must have eyes to see what happens here,
               How great the cost of this bleak battle is.
               Thou knowest well what talent thou dost hold
               To pilot and to lead with manner bold.   130

Turn not thy back upon thy Fate, good Han,
But turn thy heart and stay with us to fight!

HAN   What value hath reward when one is kill'd?
What benefit gives honor to the dead?
To try the fight against that station, Luke,   135
Is not good courage, rather suicide.

LUKE   Then take thou care now, Han, thou Solo act,
For certain 'tis the part thou best dost play.

HAN   Nay, listen: may the Force be with thee, Luke.

                     [Exit Luke.

The ship that flies without a thruster fails: 140
Propulsion and direction must one have
To navigate the obstacles of space.
I know 'tis true, as any pilot doth.
Then how can I imagine that a man
Can fly without a conscience as his guide?   145
Without the inner compass of my soul,
How can I vainly hope to pilot life?
I know what 'tis to choose the right and good,
I know the small Rebellion's cause is just,
I know the people here have need of help,   150
I know all this, but still do harbor doubt.
Yet shall my doubts lead me unto this choice,
And shall I choose convenience over right?
Or shall I choose myself o'er my new friends?
Aye, shall I choose rewards o'er my own soul?   155
A smuggler's heart doth keep calm time inside,
No matter sways a pirate's peaceful pulse.
But something stirs in me I ne'er have felt:
Is this a rebel's heart I feel within?

                                        [Exit Han Solo.

            Enter LUKE SKYWALKER *and* PRINCESS LEIA.

LEIA   What is the matter, Luke?
LUKE   —'Tis only Han.   160
            Methought he had a heart for good, but nay,
            He hath not chang'd his mind.
LEIA   —He hath a path
            Unto himself. Not thou, nor I, nor aught
            Can plot the course he chooses, verily.   165
LUKE   I wish as well that Ben were here with us.
LEIA   A kiss I gave thee once to give thee strength,
            Another kiss I give in friendship's hope.
                                [She kisses him, then exits.

                Enter BIGGS DARKLIGHTER.

BIGGS   Say, Luke!
LUKE   —Dear Biggs!
BIGGS   —It warms my heart to see
            Thee here, good friend. Shalt thou go with us

                                                hence   170

            Against the Empire?
LUKE   —Aye! On our return
            I'll bend thine ears with stories wild and true.

                Enter RED LEADER.

RED LEAD.   I pray thee, Luke, canst thou these ships control?

BIGGS	I'll stand as witness, Sir, that Luke shall prove
	More worthy than myself. I'll warrant he's 175
	The best of pilots in the Outer Rim.
	Fear not this one, good Sir, he'll earn his way.
RED LEAD.	Good lad, thou shalt suffice.
LUKE	—Aye, merry, Sir,
	I'll do my part.

[Red Leader exits.

BIGGS	—Now must we thither go.
	But when we come again unto this place, 180
	I'll drink with thee a dram of Naboo's ale
	Whilst thou thy tales relate.
LUKE	—Say, Biggs, take note:
	For once I did assure thee I would join
	Rebellion's ranks, and here am I e'en now.
BIGGS	Shall be like olden times on Tatooine. 185
	Dear friend, it gives me comfort for to see
	Thee here. E'en death could come and welcome be,
	Because I know that thou dost ride beside.

[Exit Biggs. Luke ascends to ship, with R2-D2
and rebel chief.

CHIEF	This R2 unit hath known better days.
	Wouldst thou a fit replacement for it find? 190
R2-D2	[*aside:*] Thou knave, say'st thou I have known
	better days?
	I'll better my days yet upon thy pate!
LUKE	Nay, say not so! For R2 hath been mine
	Through many an adventure and, belike,
	Hath exploits still to undergo.
R2-D2	—Beep, squeak! 195

Enter C-3PO.

C-3PO   O be thou safe, dear R2, and return!
               For thou wouldst not that my existence should
               Become a bore! [*Aside:*] O Fate, I prithee, keep
               Them safe—my Master and my only friend—
               Else should I find a lonely, tragic end.   200

                                        [*Exeunt.*

SCENE 5.

Space. The final battle.

CHORUS   As our scene shifts to space, so deep and dark,
                O'er your imagination we'll hold sway.
                For neither players nor the stage can mark
                The great and mighty scene they must portray.
                We ask you, let your keen mind's eye be chief—   5
                Think when we talk of starships, there they be.
                If you can soon suspend thy disbelief,
                The Death Star battle shall you plainly see!
                So now: the preparation made with care,
                Toward the Death Star rides the noble fleet.   10
                By whirr of engines rebels take the air,
                With courage strong their unknown Fate to meet.

Enter LUKE SKYWALKER, R2-D2, WEDGE ANTILLES,
BIGGS DARKLIGHTER, RED LEADER, GOLD LEADER, *and other*
pilots, each standing in a different place to represent his ship.
C-3PO, PRINCESS LEIA, *and* GENERAL DODONNA *stand aside.*

COMPUTER   The Death Star doth approach, and shall within
            The range of Yavin's rebel base arrive
            Within these fifteen minutes. Lo! Alert!   15
RED LEAD.   Good men, each now shall speak and state his name.
RED TEN   Red Ten doth here stand by.
RED SEVEN   —Red Seven doth
            Stand by.
BIGGS   —Red Three doth here stand by.
RED SIX   —Red Six
            Doth here stand by.
RED NINE   —Red Nine doth here stand by.
WEDGE   Red Two doth here stand by.
RED ELEVEN   —Red Eleven   20
            Doth here stand by.
LUKE   —Red Five doth here stand by.
            [*Aside:*] We have our numbers, yet our souls
                                            have names.

            For I am Luke Skywalker, here beside
            My friends, good Biggs and Wedge Antilles, too—
            No war shall render us unto mere threes   25
            And twos and fives. We ride, for ride we must—
            And here we ride in Ben's most worthy name,
            True, here we ride in Leia's noble name,
            Aye, here we ride in Alderaan's slain name—
            O here we ride for all the names which have,   30
            Throughout our lives, been written on our hearts.
            Our debt to them is past all numbering.
RED LEAD.   Now lock thine S foils in attacking mode.
            We shall pass through the thin magnetic field.
            Use your deflector shields and form in line!   35

I prithee, men, take care and be ye bold.

WEDGE   But look, I say, how large this Death Star is!
               [*Aside:*] I am afear'd that this shall be my end.

RED LEAD.   Pray, peace, Red Two! Now all accelerate
               Unto the speed wherein we may attack.   40
               The time is here, good men, 'tis not to come:
               It will be now. The readiness is all.

GOLD LEAD.   Red Leader, dost thou hear me?

RED LEAD.   —Verily.

GOLD LEAD.   The Gold Team leads unto the target shaft.

RED LEAD.   We have a positive position reach'd,   45
               Thus shall I fly across the axis for
               To draw their fire whilst thou dost penetrate.

CHORUS   The rebel ships now make their first attack
               And fire unto the Death Star's iron walls.
               The Empire shoots with lethal laser back: 50
               'Tis death to anyone on whom it falls.

WEDGE   The volleys fall from close at hand.

RED LEAD.   —I see!

LUKE   Red Five reporting: swiftly I go in!
               [*Aside:*] My first attempt here falls—O hit the mark!

CHORUS   With courage rare Luke makes initial pass   55
               And blasts his way unto the Death Star's hull.
               But now maneuvers he too close, alas!
               Shall he escape the fire's most deadly pull?

BIGGS   How goes it, Luke?

LUKE   —I nearly cook'd my goose,
               But all is well. [*Aside:*] Now shall I take more care!   60

Enter DARTH VADER *and* OFFICER 5, *aside.*

OFFICER 5	Full thirty ships descend upon us, Sir.
	So small are they our lasers pass them by.
VADER	Aye, then shall we destroy them ship to ship.
	Tell thou the crews "be ready to attack."

       [Exeunt Darth Vader and Officer 5.

RED LEAD.	Now take ye care, good men! Great fire doth rage	65
	From outside of the harsh deflection tow'r.	
LUKE	I stand prepar'd.	
BIGGS	—Now shall I strike! Pray, give	
	Me thy good cover, Porkins.	
RED SIX	—Stand I strong	
	And ready for to give thee aid, Red Three.	
CHORUS	Now bravely Biggs doth render sharp, hard blast	70
	Unto the evil Death Star's armor'd side.	
	The Empire's fire unto his mate hath pass'd,	
	And now Red Six doth face a troubl'd ride.	
RED SIX	Disaster at me strikes.	
BIGGS	—Eject, forsooth!	
RED SIX	I yet may set it right.	
BIGGS	—Anon, pull up!	75
RED SIX	Nay, nay, I'll warrant that all shall be well—	

       [Explosion. Red Six dies.

COMPUTER	In seven minutes shall the Death Star be	
	Within the range of our fair rebel base.	
CHORUS	As rebels' spirits with great strength redound,	
	A voice speaks unto Luke, as to a son.	
	Luke hears the voice and its familiar sound:	80
	'Tis his old friend and Master Obi-Wan.	

Enter GHOST OF OBI-WAN KENOBI.

GHOST   [*aside:*] Pray, trust thy feelings, Luke.

LUKE   —I hear this voice
And know it well. O me! Speak thou again!
And heed the voice, my soul, and trust thyself:
On Ben's command I'll strike a hearty blow!   85
> [*He shoots and strikes Death Star.*
> *Exit Ghost of Obi-Wan Kenobi.*

Enter CONTROL OFFICER.

OFFICER   Squad leaders, mark me well. New fighters have
Appear'd, and come toward you presently.

LUKE   My scope shows naught, my eyes to them are blind.

RED LEAD.   Employ thy visu'l scanning—they approach!
Red Seven, thou hast one upon thy rear.   90

RED SEVEN My ship is hit! Now must I die, dear friends.
> [*Explosion. Red Seven dies.*

LUKE   Good friends, if thou dost catch an enemy
Behind thy ship, I prithee watch it well!

BIGGS   Now am I plagued by such a one, help help!
For neither can I see where he doth go—   95
He flies so close that my maneuvers fail.

LUKE   Hold fast, brave Biggs, till I can give thee aid.
Upon the enemy I fly, and shoot!

BIGGS   Bold Luke, thou hast a life return'd to me.
So may I one day give to thee in turn.   100

Enter DARTH VADER *with* IMPERIAL PILOTS 1 *and* 2.

VADER   I prithee, soldiers, let us hence away.

For many of our fighters are remov'd
From their own fleet. Thus let us swiftly go
And straightway make pursuit of these rogue ships.
                              [Darth Vader and pilots enter ships.
BIGGS   O Luke, thou art pursued, pull in!
WEDGE   —Pray, guard   105
                 Thy back, good Luke. More fighters do approach.
LUKE   I have been hit, but not unto the death.
                 Small R2, see if thou the damage canst
                 Repair.
R2-D2   —Beep, whistle.
LUKE   —Hang thou on, good droid!
RED LEAD.   Red Ten, canst thou see whither's gone Red Five?   110
RED TEN   A heavy fire appears upon this side.
                 Red Five, where art thou?
LUKE   —Here, but cannot shake
                 The villain who doth hotly follow me.
WEDGE   I come for thee, good Luke, be not afraid.
LUKE   [*aside:*] O fie, my dear friend Biggs, where
                                          canst thou be?   115
                 Thou promis'd that thou ow'dst to me a life,
                 But where is now that help of which thou spok'st?
                 'Twas partly for our friendship I am here,
                 For long I wish'd to join thee as thou fought
                 And many were the tales adventurous   120
                 Thou brought'st with thee whilst visiting our home
                 When still I worked the crops on Tatooine.
                 But now hast thou deserted me, old friend?
                 When I am even at the door of death
                 Hast thou both flown and fled? Say nay, dear Biggs!   125

WEDGE	Take that, thou scoundrel base, Imperi'l scum!
LUKE	Great thanks, good Wedge, heroic'lly hast thou done.
GOLD LEAD.	Red Leader, hear my word: the Gold team shall
	Begin our swift attack into the trench.
RED LEAD.	Godspeed, Gold Leader, go with might and strength! 130
VADER	I fly, and fly toward my enemies.
	This day the dark side of the Force shall reign,
	As I disrupt the weak Rebellion's plans
	And with my men destroy their ev'ry hope.
	[To Imperial Pilots 1 and 2:] Good pilots both,
	remain set for attack! 135
GOLD LEAD.	The port for the exhaust hath been lock'd in
	And mark'd! That hole shall make us whole,
	my mates.
	Now switch thy pow'r to front deflector screens.
	Gold Five, what say'st thou? Canst thou count
	the guns?
GOLD FIVE	Belike 'tis twenty yon and hither, both 140
	Upon the surface and within the tow'rs.
COMPUTER	Within five minutes shall the Death Star be
	Upon our rebel base, and set to strike.
GOLD LEAD.	To targeting computer presently
	I switch.
GOLD TWO	—I have receiv'd a signal on 145
	The ship's computer—that the port will soon
	Be in our range. But soft, good friends, what's this?
	The guns! It seemeth that their guns have stopp'd.
GOLD FIVE	So watch thy rear, and stabilize thy shields.
	Perhaps an enemy doth come behind. 150
GOLD LEAD.	Aye, aye, they come! Three ships at point-two-ten.

CHORUS   The battle heats as Vader and his men
                Approach the threefold members of group Gold.
                The Empire's hate will be fulfillèd when
                Darth makes his power known with blows
                                                full bold. 155

VADER   I shall destroy the rebels vile myself.
                Just give me thy good cover and 'tis done.
                Now shoot I once, and death is the result.
                        [Darth Vader shoots. Explosion. Gold Two dies.

GOLD LEAD. I have no power to maneuver, fie!
GOLD FIVE   Stay thou on target.
GOLD LEAD.   —Nay, we run too close!   160
GOLD FIVE   Stay thou on target!
GOLD LEAD.   —Wretch, pray give me room!
                            [Darth Vader shoots. Explosion.
                                        Gold Leader dies.

GOLD FIVE   Gold Five doth this ill news report: we have
                Lost Dutch and Tiree both.
RED LEAD.   —In troth, I hear!
                Stay ready.
GOLD FIVE   —From behind they do attack!
                        [Darth Vader shoots. Explosion. Gold Five dies.

LUKE   [aside:] So much of desolation and of death.   165
                Is this Rebellion worth the lives here lost?
                Yet I would gladly my life give to it—
                Thus reason not the need, my troubl'd soul.

CHORUS   Whilst all the rebels mourn the loss of life,
                Upon the Death Star tensions have been prov'd.   170
                The rebels' plan hath rear'd the threat of strife,
                But Gov'nor Tarkin stands assur'd, unmov'd.

Enter GRAND MOFF TARKIN *with* CHIEF OFFICER *aside,*
in Death Star.

CH. OFFICER   The rebels' sharp attack hath been well prob'd
              And now it doth appear a danger looms.
              I do confess my love to thee, good Sir,   175
              And would my very life lay down for thee.
              Wouldst thou that I make ready thine own ship,
              That thou may'st flee should fighting turn to death?
TARKIN   Retreat whilst we do win the day? You jest!
              Forsooth, I stand unmovèd like a rock.   180
                    [Exeunt Grand Moff Tarkin and Chief Officer.
COMPUTER   The Death Star shall within three minutes be
              Upon the rebel base.
RED LEAD.   —Red boys, 'tis I,
              Thy tried and true Red Leader. We shall meet
              Upon the mark at six-point-one. Make haste!
WEDGE   Red Two doth stand obedi'nt at thy side.   185
BIGGS   Red Three doth come.
DODONNA   —Red Leader, hear me now.
              It is Base One who speaks to thee. Keep half
              Thy fighters out of range upon thy next
              Attempt. If one group sadly falls, belike
              The other shall succeed: so shall we make   190
              The Empire take our fleet by halves, not wholes.
RED LEAD.   I hear and understand, good Sir. Now Luke,
              Take thou Red Two and Three with thee and wait
              Upon my signal ere thou mak'st thy run.
              Now hence we go an Empire for to slay!   195
CHORUS   Red Leader, with the others, Twelve and Ten,

Make their descent into the trench with speed.
Their brav'ry, cunning, and their acumen
May give these men the victory they need.

RED TEN   Dost thou agree, it should be in our sights?   200

RED LEAD.   Pray keep thine eyes a'watching for those ships
That have our comrades cruelly destroy'd!

RED TEN   The interference hath become too wide.
Red Five, canst thou yet see them where thou standst?

LUKE   I see no ships, but—wait. Aye, they approach!   205
They come at point-three-five.

RED TEN   —I see them now.

RED LEAD.   My ship hath come in range of that sly port,
The port that hath evaded us so far.
But now, aye now, the target shall be mine.
If ye, good friends, may hold them there awhile,   210
I shall this battle end with one swift stroke!

VADER   Close in, my lads—we three shall ride as one.

RED LEAD.   Heigh, almost there.

                    [Darth Vader shoots. Explosion. Red Twelve dies.

RED TEN   —Pray fire, else we die too!

RED LEAD.   Heigh, almost there.

RED TEN   —They set upon my back!
I can no more withstand their quick attack.   215

                    [Darth Vader shoots. Explosion. Red Ten dies.

RED LEAD.   I shoot, I shoot! For rebels' glory, shoot!
The blast hath left the shaft!

RED NINE   —Hast hit? Hast hit?
Is vict'ry yet within our sights?

RED LEAD.   —Alas,
My finest effort I have giv'n, and yet,

	The blast falls errant and doth miss the mark.	220
	'Tis but an impact on the surface. Pooh!	
LUKE	Red Leader, be thou not dismay'd. We shall	
	Protect thee even now. Turn thou toward	
	The point-oh-five and we shall cover thee.	
RED LEAD.	Nay, save me not! My engine hath been crush'd	225
	And death is welcome now. Instead, dear Luke,	
	Good Wedge, brave Biggs, be thou preparèd for	
	Thy run, for thou art now our only hope!	

   [Darth Vader shoots. Explosion. Red Leader dies.

COMPUTER	The Death Star now in but a minute shall	
	Upon the rebel base on Yavin come.	230
LUKE	Once more unto the trench, dear friends, once more!	
	The death of our dear friends we see today,	
	And by my troth their souls shall be aveng'd!	
	I was not angry since I came to space	
	Until this instant! Strike at us and thou	235
	Shalt know the power of the Force, thou brute,	
	Thou Empire full of hate and evil deeds.	
	Aye, pluck us down and we shall rise again—	
	Our cause is not alone for these good men	
	Who here were kill'd today. Our cause is not	240
	Alone for those on Alderaan who died.	
	Our cause is for the truth, for righteousness,	
	For anyone who e'er oppression knew.	
	'Tis not rebellion for the sake of one,	
	'Tis not a cause to serve a priv'leg'd few—	245
	This moment shall resound in history	
	For ev'ry person who would freedom know!	
	So Biggs, stand with me now, and be my aide,	

	And Wedge, fly at my side to lead the charge—	
	We three, we happy three, we band of brothers,	250
	Shall fly unto the trench with throttles full!	
WEDGE	We stand with thee, a'ready for the fight.	
BIGGS	But Luke, at that quick pace shalt thou escape	
	Before thy speedy ship is blown in twain?	
LUKE	'Twill be like Beggars Canyon back at home.	255
CHORUS	The youth descend at once into the trench	
	Wherein their fates shall surely written be.	
	Darth Vader, close behind, prepares to quench	
	His thirst upon the blood of martyrs three.	
BIGGS	We shall stand fast at hand to give thee help.	260
WEDGE	My scope doth show the tower, but the port	
	Appeareth not. How certain art thou, Luke,	
	That our computers each can hit the mark?	
LUKE	Good pilot, watch thyself! Increase to full.	
WEDGE	I prithee, what shall we do 'bout the tow'r?	265
LUKE	Give thou unto the enemy thy thoughts,	
	But let the tow'r be my concern alone.	
	[To R2-D2:] Now R2, fix the stabilizer that	
	Hath once more come unhing'd. Pray, fix it fast!	
R2-D2	[aside:] Now shall I be not fool, but fix!	
	[To Luke:] Beep, squeak!	270
WEDGE	The fighters are behind us, at point-three.	
	They come upon my rear too fast. Alack!	
	I have been hit, and must depart, my friends.	
LUKE	Aye, get thee clear, good Wedge. Thou shalt not help	
	Our cause if thy ship flyeth not. Anon!	275
	And live to fight another day with me.	
WEDGE	With all my heart, I truly wish thee well.	

[Exit Wedge.

VADER   Aye, let him go—the leader we pursue!

BIGGS   Make haste, O Luke. Methinks they do approach
               E'en faster than before. I shall not hold   280
               Them back for long!

LUKE   —Now, R2, straight increase
               The pow'r.

R2-D2   —Beep, whee.

BIGGS   —Make haste, Luke. O, alas!
               [Darth Vader shoots. Explosion. Biggs dies.

LUKE   That ever I should see this day, O woe!
               My childhood friend from Tatooine now slain
               Protecting me from harm. Thou ow'dst a life—   285
               Dear Biggs, sweet Biggs—and thou hast paid. And now
               'Tis down to me: the boy turn'd warrior.
               Be still, my errant heart, and seek the Force.

VADER   The leader now is mine.

R2-D2   —Meep, beep.

C-3PO   —Take care
               Sweet R2-D2! Come thou back, I pray!   290

CHORUS   Luke's ship comes closer to the little port
               While Vader and his crew draw all too near.
               Young Luke to his computer doth resort
               Until he hears the voice speak in his ear.

               Enter GHOST OF OBI-WAN KENOBI.

GHOST	O use the Force, dear Luke. Let go and trust!	295
VADER	I sense the Force in this one here, almost	
	As if I did my younger self espy.	
GHOST	I prithee, trust me, Luke. All shall be well.	
LUKE	The hearing of these words is like a balm	
	Unto my soul. So shall I trust the Force	300
	And not this fallible computer here.	

[Luke turns off computer.

COMPUTER	What is this, Luke? Thy targeting machine
	Hath been turn'd off. What can be wrong? Pray tell!
LUKE	Nay, all is well. Fear not, good friends.
R2-D2	—Beep, squeak.

[Darth Vader shoots. R2-D2 is hit.

Ahh hoo!

LUKE	—Small R2-D2 hath been lost!	305
COMPUTER	The Death Star now has come within our range.	
TARKIN	Commander, thou may'st fire when thou hast made	
	All goodly preparation thereunto.	
VADER	Now face thy death, thou rebel.	
PILOT	—Sir, take heed!	
CHORUS	Now in a trice brave Han is on the scene!	310
	The smuggler hath return'd on errand kind.	
	With sly approach he makes his way unseen	
	And slays th'Imperi'l pilots from behind.	

[Enter Han Solo with Chewbacca, firing on
Darth Vader and Imperial Pilots. Explosion.
Imperial Pilots 1 and 2 die.

VADER	But how?—

[Darth Vader exits in confusion, his ship spinning
out of control.

HAN   —Thy path is clear, young Luke. Now do
            Thy deed and let us all make way back home.   315

LUKE   I stretch my feelings out and use the Force,
            And on the instant seems the porthole vast—
            Not small or difficult to strike, but large.
            The ship is arm'd, and now I take the chance—
            The blast's away, and with it all our hopes!   320
                       [Luke shoots and hits the target.

CHORUS   The laser hits its mark with certain aim,
           And as the Death Star arms to strike the base
           The chain reaction sets the orb aflame:
           The Death Star hath exploded into space.
HAN   Thy timely blast hath hit the perfect mark—   325
           One in a million was thy Force-fill'd shot!
GHOST   Remember me, O Luke, remember me,
           And ever shall the Force remain with thee.

                                        [*Exeunt.*

SCENE 6.

The rebel base on Yavin IV.

Enter LUKE SKYWALKER *from ship, with* PRINCESS LEIA
and various rebels.

REBELS   Hurrah!
LUKE   —O Leia!
LEIA   —Luke! Thou didst succeed!

Enter HAN SOLO.

HAN   Heigh-ho!
LUKE   —Good friend! I knew thou wouldst return.
           I knew thou must, 'twas in thy spirit good.
HAN   Nay, should a pirate let another take
           His own reward?
LEIA   —Thou gentle soul, I knew   5
           Thou wert of sterner stuff than money made.

Enter R2-D2, *injured, and* C-3PO.

C-3PO   O R2, R2, canst thou hear me? Speak!
          Canst thou repair him? Say thou canst, I beg!
          If any of my parts may be of use,
          Pray say the word!
LUKE   —Fear not, he'll be made whole.   10
REBEL 2   We shall at once begin our best repair.
                    [*Exeunt C-3PO with R2-D2 and Rebel Leader 2.*
LUKE   Now ends a noble quest, a battle won.
          Now hath a true adventure reach'd its goal.
          Now hath the good Rebellion fac'd its foe
          And triumph'd though it seem'd that all was lost.   15
LEIA   Along the way, dear friends were lost and made,
          Along the way, strange creatures have we found.
          The stories have been told, the villains met,
          The griefs and exultations all play'd out.
HAN   A chance for new beginnings we have made,   20
          Directing hearts unto the rebels' cause.
          These are the star wars we have fought and won—
          For now our battles and our scenes are done.

Enter CHORUS *as epilogue.*

CHORUS   Now dawns a new day with the sun of Peace,
          The day whereon the rebels welcome Fate.   25
          For from their enemies they find release
          And now with mirth they come to celebrate.
          Young Luke, strong in the Force, doth walk beside
          The noble Han, whose valor won the day.

The rebels form an aisle and rise with pride,　　30
As Luke and Han march forth in grand display.
Now Leia smiles and gives them their reward,
As each bows low with hope and joy sincere.
C-3PO and R2, now restor'd,
Look on as brave Chewbacca sounds the cheer.　　35
There let our heroes rest free from attack,
Till darkness rise and Empire striketh back.

[Exeunt omnes.

END.

AFTERWORD.

William Shakespeare's Star Wars.

At first glance, the title seems absurd.

But there's a surprising and very real connection between George Lucas's cinematic masterpiece and the thirty-seven (give or take) plays of William Shakespeare. That connection is a man named Joseph Campbell, author of the landmark book *The Hero with a Thousand Faces.*

Campbell was famous for his pioneering work as a mythologist. He studied legends and myths from throughout world history to identify the recurring elements—or archetypes—that power all great storytelling. Through his research, Campbell discovered that certain archetypes appeared again and again in narratives separated by hundreds of years, from ancient Greek mythologies to classic Hollywood westerns. Naturally, the plays of William Shakespeare were an important source for Campbell's scholarship, with brooding prince Hamlet among his cadre of archetypal heroes.

George Lucas was among the first filmmakers to consciously apply Campbell's scholarship to motion pictures. "In reading *The Hero with a Thousand Faces,*" he told Campbell's biographers, "I began to realize that my first draft of *Star Wars* was following classic motifs . . . so I modified my next draft according to what I'd been learning about classical motifs and made it a little bit more consistent."

To put it more simply, Campbell studied Shakespeare to produce *The Hero with a Thousand Faces,* and Lucas studied Campbell to produce *Star Wars*. So it's not at all surprising that the *Star Wars* saga features archetypal characters and relationships similar to those found in Shakespearean drama. The complicated parent/child relationship of Darth Vader/Luke Skywalker (and the mentor/student relationship of Obi-Wan Kenobi/Luke Skywalker) recalls plays like *Henry IV Parts 1 and 2*, *The Tempest*, and *Hamlet*. Like Sith lords, many of Shakespeare's villains are easily identifiable and almost entirely evil, with notable baddies including Iago (*Othello*), Edmund (*King Lear*), and Don John (*Much Ado about Nothing*). Still others, like Darth Vader, are more conflicted and complex in their malevolence: *Hamlet*'s Claudius and the band of conspirators in *Julius Caesar*. Destiny and fate are key themes of *Star Wars*, as they are in *Romeo and Juliet*, *A Midsummer Night's Dream*, and *Macbeth*.

Shakespeare's plays and *Star Wars* also feature a host of colorful supporting players. C-3PO and R2-D2 observe and comment on the action like Rosencrantz and Guildenstern. Chewbacca is as untamable as Caliban. Lando is as smooth and self-interested (at first) as Brutus. Obi-Wan Kenobi is like a wise Prospero (before death) or a haunting King Hamlet (after). Jabba the Hutt enjoys a diet worthy of Falstaff. Boba Fett is like *Richard III*'s murderers 1, 2, and 3, but with a jetpack and blaster instead of a knife. Yoda's speech is as backward as Dogberry's but as wise as Polonius's.

The works of Shakespeare and the *Star Wars* movies also share a comparable level of popularity and relevance. All well-rounded postmodern cultural connoisseurs are expected to have at least passing familiarity with both sets of stories, and both have percolated into our everyday language: you're as likely to hear one of Shakespeare's enduring phrases ("good riddance," "faint-hearted," "elbow room," and many others) as an encouragement to "use the force." If *Star Wars* were an actual Shakespearean play, we would most likely classify it as a fantasy, in the vein of *The Tempest*. However, it also has elements of a history (the story of the Galactic Empire with all the intrigue of *Richard III*), a comedy (all's well that ends well, after all), or, taken as a six-movie arc, the Tragedy of Anakin Skywalker.

I had the idea for *William Shakespeare's Star Wars* after watching the original trilogy for the millionth time and (soon afterward) attending four shows at the Oregon Shakespeare Festival. I'd already committed every scene and speech of the *Star Wars* saga to memory, but the Shakespeare festival introduced me to something new: *The Very Merry Wives of Windsor, Iowa,* an adaptation by Alison Carey of the classic comedy set in contemporary Iowa among a populace happily embracing gay marriage. I saw the appeal of applying the Shakespearean tradition to surprising and nontraditional story elements, and the next morning I woke up with the idea for this book.

My interests in language and wordplay came in handy while attempting to translate so much classic movie dialogue into iambic pentameter. For those unfamiliar with the phrase, iambic pentameter is the metrical form that Shakespeare uses in his plays and sonnets. An *iamb* is the syllable pattern unstressed-stressed, and *pentameter* means each line has five iambs, so a line of iambic pentameter sounds like this: da-DUM da-DUM da-DUM da-DUM da-DUM (Simon and Garfunkel's "I'd rather be a hammer than a nail" is a perfect example). The rhythm of iambic pentameter feels natural and intuitive to me, so I had a lot of fun writing 3,076 lines of it. Geeky trivia: this puts *William Shakespeare's Star Wars* at an average length for a Shakespearean play (*A Comedy of Errors* is the shortest, at 1,786 lines; *Hamlet* is the longest, at 4,024).

This has been a labor of love, and I've enjoyed every syllable.

ACKNOWLEDGMENTS.

The process of writing this, my first book, has been a thrilling journey into the publishing world, and I am grateful to all those who made the way clear. Thank you to Jason Rekulak, my editor at Quirk Books, for believing in this book and for encouraging me to write it in the first place. Thank you to Adriann Ranta, my agent, for guiding me through the maze of contracts and answering the thousand questions of a first-time author. Thanks to both Jennifer Heddle and Carol Roeder at Lucasfilm for making the editorial process a smooth one, to Nicolas Delort for his amazing illustrations, and to the rest of the Quirk and Lucasfilm staff for their wonderful contributions.

Great thanks to my literal and metaphorical brothers Erik Doescher, Josh Hicks, and Ethan Youngerman for being early readers of the manuscript and constant cheerleaders along the way. Thank you to my parents, Beth and Bob Doescher, for their unconditional love and for making *Star Wars* a part of my reality since before I can remember.

Profound thanks to Murray Biggs, my college English professor and good friend. Murray performed a Herculean task for this book, poring over the manuscript and making minor corrections to improve my Shakespearean pastiche (and teaching me the word *pastiche*). Thank you to Jane Bidwell, my high school English teacher, for instilling in me a love of Shakespeare and an understanding of iambic pentameter.

Additional thanks to others who offered help and support: Heidi Altman, Jeff and Caryl Creswell, Mark Fordice, Holly Havens, Jim and Nancy Hicks, Apricot Irving, Steve Maddoux, Chris Martin, Matt Matros, Joan and Grady Miller, Michael Morrill, Dave Nieuwstraten, Naomi Walcott, and Doug Zabroski.

Finally, thank you to my spouse, Jennifer Creswell, and our children Liam and Graham. Though not a lover of Shakespeare—and possessing a general antipathy toward *Star Wars*—Jennifer has shown support, love, and encouragement throughout the development of this book. Liam and Graham have been excited about "daddy's book" from the start and (he notes with pride) have become big *Star Wars* fans in the process.

SONNET 1138

"To the Interwebs We Go"

Our rebels now are ended, but fear not—
The book is over, true, but not th'event.
For there's an online Shakespeare *Star Wars* spot
Where thou may'st soon prolong thy merriment.
One may download a gratis **study guide**
Design'd for high school or for college classes,
And there's an **interview** to be espied
With author Ian Doescher, for the masses.
The mem'ry of the book shall live again
When thou, with joy, shalt our **book trailer** see,
Or read o'er any news that shall come in
About the Shakespeare *Star Wars* galaxy.
All this **and more**, aye, surely thou shalt find,
When thou dost visit good **Quirk Books online**.

quirkbooks.com/shakespearestarwars